It Is
What
It Is!

Universal and
everlasting lessons
from lockdown

To Laura
Love & Light
Marie Claire
xx

It Is What It Is!

Universal and everlasting lessons from lockdown

Marie-Claire Donnelly

London

It Is What It Is! Universal and everlasting lessons from lockdown

The book information is catalogued as follows;
Author Name(s): Marie-Claire Donnelly
Title: It Is What It Is! Universal and everlasting lessons from lockdown
Description; First Edition
1st Edition, 2020

Book Design by Leah Kent

ISBN 978-1-913479-79-4 (paperback)
ISBN 978-1-913479-80-0 (ebook)

Published by That Guy's House
www.ThatGuysHouse.com

For Craig, Ciaran, Maria and Charlotte –
you saved me!

Introduction:
BC (Before Coronavirus)

....

I the Lord of sea and sky
I have heard my people cry
All who dwell in dark and sin
My hand will save
I have made the stars of night
I will make their darkness bright
Who will bear my light to them?
Whom shall I send?

Here I am Lord
Is it I Lord?
I have heard You calling in the night
I will go, Lord
If You lead me
I will hold Your people in my heart

'They' say everyone has a book in them, and I have
desperately wanted to write a book for most of my life. I have
dabbled, have started a few and even finished one, but none of
them has ever felt right or good enough. Maybe it was just me
that didn't feel 'right' or 'good enough'.

I love writing, and always have. I was the geek who loved
English at school and spent my lunchtimes in the library
drafting and re-drafting my assignments. The girl who swelled
with pride when my English teacher, Mrs Burns, praised my
efforts and gave me a good mark.

'What is the book that you are most afraid to write?' is a classic coaching question, and when my coach asked me this, I was initially confused, until recently. I thought, 'How could anyone be afraid to write a book? What does that question even mean?'

Then I received 'my calling' to write this book – and it scared the hell out of me.

For what reason was I so scared? How can something I love doing and am so passionate about make me feel scared?

It is because, for all of my life, I have been ashamed of my faith, of the deep belief that I have in God. I have played it down, pretended to my peers that it is not that important to me, and I have even denied it on occasion (being a Scottish Catholic is not fun at times). I have been terrified of being judged because of it and felt like I wouldn't 'fit in' if I spoke about how connected I feel to God.

As a result, I hid my faith in a box and only brought it out when no-one else was around or when I was in the company of a few people who I understood to feel the same way as me.

The book that I was scared to write, therefore, is about my connection to God and how I have been guided all my life by my interpretation of His teachings. It is my firm hope that anyone who reads this book will learn (or be reminded of) the same lessons I was taught during the lockdown period. The period of time where we were all made to stop and were given an opportunity to reflect, change, and adapt to a new way of being.

Re-learning or being reminded of these valuable lessons has enabled me to suffer less during this lockdown period and reemerge from it onto a path of deep inner peace and happiness, living a life of abundance in all senses of the word. I am hopeful that if everyone takes the time to reflect and subsequently learn the lessons, then there will be a whole lot less suffering in the world.

We will thrive, as opposed to survive. As God intended for us all.

In a world where we are expected to be, do, and have it all (which can be completely and utterly draining) making a return to faith, love, acceptance, and forgiveness will benefit us all mentally, emotionally, and physically.

Prior to lockdown, I believed that this world was moving so far away from God's wish for us all that it seemed like it might never be achieved. It was impossible.

So many of us berate our bodies and our minds – we abuse ourselves mentally and physically. We judge others, we bitch, gossip, compare, compete, and put others down to make ourselves feel better. We inadvertently destroy this beautiful planet which we are blessed to live on through our actions – every single day.

There has to be another way – and there is. God's way.

I digress – back to this 'calling' I received. Even writing this still makes me cringe – my inner critic is doing her happy dance right now, singing 'Who Do You Think You Are?' in the style of the Spice Girls and asking, 'Out of everyone on this planet, why would God call on YOU?'

I am, however, getting so much better at bringing awareness to my inner critic, and, rather than disliking her, I have learned to send her love and thank her for trying to protect me in the only way that she knows. We have become much better friends, and our relationship is getting better and better with each passing day.

Deep in my heart, I know that I was called by God and that I had a job to do. I also know that I am completely and utterly committed to stepping up and doing it to the very best of my ability.

My journey started BC (Before Coronavirus – shameful play on words). I was away for a fun weekend in Rome at the end of January 2020 with my mum and two sisters. We had enjoyed a brilliant couple of days exploring Rome and sampling the local cuisine, which mainly consisted of Aperol Spritz, pizza, and tiramisu.

On the third day of our trip, we had planned a tour of the Vatican Museum followed by a visit to St Peter's Square and the Basilica. My Mum, Joanna and I were BUZZING. Gillian, not so much, on account of the fact that she was 'all holy place-d' out and said, 'If you have seen one Chapel, you have seen them all.'

After the tour of the Vatican Museum, the four of us were walking down the street heading towards St Peters Square. We bore an uncanny resemblance to the Teletubbies on account of us all wearing brightly coloured ponchos which we had recently purchased from a street vendor, as it was raining when we left the Vatican Museum.

We were all giggling and laughing at how ridiculous we looked and how we had managed to bag ourselves a bargain as the vendor selling them only charged five euros for them all when it was supposed to be five euros each (Scottish people love a bargain).

Upon reflection, this should have been the first sign that our day was going to be incredible – you almost never get a bargain from a person trying to sell overpriced ponchos in Rome!! Especially when it is raining!

Out of nowhere, it seemed, a man stepped directly into our path and asked, 'Are you ladies Scottish?' We looked at the man. He was standing on the path leading to St Peter's Square. He was a regular looking guy, dressed normal, so normal I cannot remember exactly what he was wearing nor what he looked like. We assumed that he was a tour guide. He had an English accent, and I mentally noted that he was the first English-speaking guide we had encountered during our trip. I then dismissed this observation, thinking nothing more about it.

'Aye,' we confirmed in our best broad Scottish accent. (It's got to be done, hasn't it?)

'Where are you heading?' the man asked. We rolled our eyes and assumed a sales pitch was coming on.

'To St Peter's Square and the Basilica,' we replied. Eh, duh! Where else would we be going?

'You can't, it closed at 12.30 pm, you will have to come back later,' he said and then left us to it. Strange – no sell – we thought.

Taking him at his word, we thanked him and decided to go for lunch instead. As we headed away from him, Joanna and I exchanged a cynical 'I am not buying it' look with each other and decided to google 'St Peter's Square opening hours' while we were at lunch.

As we suspected, it hadn't closed for the day. That guy!!! What was that all about? Why would he say that? We ordered drinks and food and soon forgot about his motives and decided to head up to St Peter's after lunch. Reflecting on this, I now believe that it was divine intervention. We were not meant to be at St Peter's Square at the time we had planned. It was destined for us to go later.

On arriving at St Peter's Square, we noticed that there were two queues, one long, one short. Now, being of the belief that life is too short to queue (a belief hardwired into the neural pathways of my mind after a two-hour wait for a ninety-second attraction in Universal Studios, Florida) I said, 'Come on, we have fast passes (we actually did), let's join this queue.'

The queue to which I was referring consisted of a group of giggling nuns taking selfies with their fellow nun friends. They were the cutest nuns I have ever had the pleasure of meeting. Each of them was waving bright red tickets about their heads and were off-the-scale hyper about going into the Basilica. The energy was electric around them, and we tapped into the excitement that was radiating off of them.

One thing we did note, however, was that we were not in possession of the red tickets that the nuns had, but we decided to go with the flow and followed the giggling nuns as the queue got closer to security.

What happened next still feels a bit surreal: it was as if we had donned invisibility cloaks which enabled us to glide easily through security, up the stairs, past the dudes in the strange stripey suits, and into the beautiful St Peter's Cathedral.

At various points during this, I thought that the gig was going to be up, and we were going to be respectfully asked to leave – especially when my sunglasses and bright red lipstick fell out of my leather jacket pocket during a security checkpoint. Not really the attire expected from a plain-clothed nun, is it?

At another security checkpoint, my sister Joanna and I looked back at my mum and Gillian in their bright pink and bright green ponchos further back in the queue, and I said to Joanna 'This will be it – we will be asked to leave.' It never happened – maybe those gifted ponchos were invisibility cloaks after all?

We never got asked to leave; instead, we were ushered into the most elaborately ornate and stunning church ever. We were offered a mass book and a candle and asked to sit towards the middle of the church amongst a congregation filled with nuns, priests, monks, and other holy looking people.

Utilising a translation app, I figured out that the mass was being said by none other than the Holy Father Pope Francis himself! I thought, 'How can this be, he wasn't supposed to be in Rome this weekend?' The excitement that I felt was off the scale and can only be compared to sitting in Madison Square Gardens, waiting for my all-time favourite legend of a singer, Billy Joel to come on stage. And just like back then, when Pope Francis walked down the aisle of that Church I did exactly the same as I did on that night in Madison Square Gardens – I burst out crying like a star-struck teenager.

I felt so incredibly happy and grateful to be there sharing this moment with my mum, who had been through so much the last few years as a result of personal illness as well as losing both hers and my dad's parents – our grandparents. She completely and utterly deserved this treat and, given that she is a massive football fan, it felt very significant that she would now have seen at least a hat-trick of Popes in her lifetime: John Paul II, Benedict, and now Francis.

I was also a bit amused at the fact that my sister Gillian, who had categorically refused to attend mass when in Rome, was going to have to sit in this church for at least an hour prior to the mass starting and then at least an hour for the actual mass itself. Her face when she realised what was happening was priceless. Sisterly banter is the best!

I love how God has such a wicked sense of humour at times.

We kept saying that someone up above must have pulling some serious strings for us to be there – and we all agreed that it was most probably Gran and Papa (my mum's parents) who both had an unshakably strong faith in God and were regular church attendees. They both also had a wicked sense of humour, and we imagined them laughing up there at the fact that Gillian had to sit in a church for two hours.

The mass, in itself, was pretty uneventful. It was in Latin, and Pope Francis was quietly-spoken and seemed very far away. What was significant, however, was the energy in the church: it seemed to vibrate with love, faith, hope, and connection. I was completely mesmerised and had this sense, an inner knowing that something significant and life-changing was happening to and for me.

It was an intuitive feeling that told me that we were meant to be there. A sense that this turn of events which brought us to be at this mass was a message from God and that he wanted us there because he had a job for us. A job that only we, maybe as a unit, maybe as individuals, were to do for him. A job that would make the world a better, more loving, connected place.

I also experienced a sense of deep inner peace and had the feeling that I was being looked after and that I always would be. This feeling was confirmed to me after the mass ended, when Joanna turned to me and said, 'Everything is going to be ok' – a bit vague I know, but I understood deep in my soul exactly what she meant. She had experienced it too.

The icing on the cake of signs came as we were exiting the church when Gillian bent down to pick up a white feather that somehow had fallen at her feet. A beautiful message, I believe, from Gran!

In the days that followed this experience, I noticed a change in myself, one that did not feel nice at all. I started to feel unsettled, disjointed, not quite my usual self – fearful even. At first, I thought it might have been as a result of the carb overload (I ate a LOT of pizza and tiramisu during that weekend) or withdrawal symptoms from Aperol Spritz (I drank a LOT of them too).

Deep down, though, I knew that it wasn't that – it was a feeling in my soul, a feeling that something had changed, a feeling that I had changed. The words 'I have encountered the Holy Spirit' (whatever the hell that meant) kept going around and around in my head. This was accompanied by a feeling that I had to DO something, something BIG.

I was scared of these feelings, really scared, I mean really, really scared. I kept asking myself WTAF was going on with me?

The scared feeling grew into one of being terrified – terrified that I was suffering from a serious mental health condition. I had recently attended a mental health first aid training course to help me to better serve my coaching clients, and I recalled that a symptom of psychosis is that the mentally ill person often believes that God is speaking to them.

Remembering this filled me with a feeling of Holy SHIT as opposed to Holy Spirit – I thought I was going to be carted off by the men in white coats, never to see my kids and husband again.

Other people then started to tell me that they were noticing something different in me – I had a light, a glow. One of my clients came right out and asked me if I had work done, as I was all that shiny way!

I did a lot of journaling and meditation in the days that followed, which settled me into these new feelings, and I started to shift from feeling terrified to accepting them to feeling really excited. I prayed and prayed for another message as to what I was to do next – all the while hoping and praying that it wasn't to up sticks in the style of leaving my fishing net and boats upon the shore to become a nun.

No offence to all those giggling nuns who helped us sneak into mass with the Holy Father. They were legends!! I just didn't want to change my life that much.

It then came to me whilst out on a morning run – my mission was to write a book. A book for ordinary people, like me, to return to what God intended for us all. A book which would allow us to feel healthier, happier, and more connected with ourselves and others.

All my life, I have been scared to speak out about my belief in God, my faith, and how I believe that I am continually receiving guidance and lessons from Him.

This is the book that I was scared to write!

Since this calling was made clear to me, the whole world has turned upside down; in the UK, it started in March 2020. God hit the pause button, and we found ourselves in the midst of a global pandemic. We were put into lockdown, being asked to adhere to very strict guidelines around what we could and could not do.

During this time, I have felt more connected to God than ever and believe that I was taught (reminded of at certain points) so many valuable lessons. These lessons are contained in the chapters that follow.

I am also so very aware that 2020 was not such an enlightening experience for so many people. As a result of the impact of this very serious, deadly virus, businesses were lost, people suffered at the hands of poor mental and physical health, and so many were unable to say goodbye or give the proper send-off to those that they loved. My heart breaks for each and every single person who was adversely affected by the virus and for the impact that it has had on the world. My love and my prayers are with them all. I am under no illusion and know that this is a deadly virus and must be taken seriously.

This book is my personal account of what the lockdown experience was like for me, the ups and downs of it all, and the silver lining I was taught to see through an extremely difficult time. I see myself as very blessed to have survived, and in some ways thrived, during the period, and I count my blessings every day for that.

Before you begin, please remember that I am a normal mum from a normal town, with a (sometimes) normal family. The lessons I received have come from normal, everyday situations that happen to us all every single day.

There are no bolts of lightning, walking on water, or turning water into wine (unfortunately).

So, in the words of a passed priest who delivered kick-ass homilies – I hope the lessons make some kind of sense.

Instructions for Reading

....

I have been brought up as a Roman Catholic, and some of the symbolism in the book refers to the Catholic faith. It is not, however, a Roman Catholic book. It is a book about having faith in something bigger than us – whether that be God, The Universe, Buddha or some other spiritual being. It is about loving ourselves, our neighbour, and our planet and with this comes the lessons of acceptance and forgiveness. It is my hope that you will receive insights regardless of your religion or lack of religion.

To get the best from the book, I recommend you use a journal as there will be questions for self-reflection at the end of each lesson. I used to be the world's worst at doing the recommended exercises when reading the works of other authors. I subsequently found myself questioning why I did not retain the insights I had. Once I became committed and made an intention to do the work and complete the exercises, it was always transformational.

The magic is in the doing. Do the exercises to gain personal insights and transformations specific to you. It will be completely worth the effort.

I also refer in the book to my training as a Quantum Energy Coach (QEC). Given that it is a relatively unknown modality, further detail is required. QEC is a form of coaching which works with the subconscious part of the mind where the power to permanently change resides. It is effective, it is safe, it is easy to do, anyone can be coached for most issues, and the results are permanent. It is a modality which combines neuroscience, cardiac coherence, focused intention and gestalt therapy. The results I have seen in both myself and my clients have been nothing short of transformational.

As a Quantum Energy Coach, I work with individuals rewiring new, better serving beliefs into the subconscious mind. The beliefs are designed as statements which are written positively and in the present tense (the subconscious mind likes this). I have included relevant belief statements at the end of each lesson. If the statements resonate, note them down and use them as daily affirmations as part of your practice. Alternatively, hook up with a Quantum Energy Coach who will work with you to install them permanently into your subconscious. A list of registered coaches can be found on www.qecliving.com

Lesson 1
Accepting and Embracing Change

....

Be not afraid,
I go before you always.
Come, follow me and I will give you rest.

Journal Entry - Early Lockdown

Dear God,

Today has been very weird!

Joanna has just dropped off some fitness equipment for me to use whilst taking part in home workouts and has collected a book that I had bought for my niece Faith. It was a very strange experience.

It was strange due to the fact that she wasn't able to come into my home, give me a cuddle, grab a coffee, and have a chat like she normally would. By chat, I mean the two of us would generally sit at my breakfast bar on our respective phones mindlessly scrolling, only half-listening to each other.

I am quickly starting to realise that all the things that I used to take for granted and maybe became a bit complacent about are going to be really hard to live without anymore. I am praying that the restrictions won't be for long. I am hopeful for a couple of weeks, three at most.

Instead of coming into my house for said coffee and social media scrolling, Joanna had to drop the fitness equipment and collect Faith's book from my front door as we aren't 'allowed' to be less than 2m near each other.

It's called 'Social Distancing' – a term that no one had ever heard of until a few weeks ago. It's a new rule that the government has enforced as a result of the Coronavirus or Covid-19 – a new virus which is spreading like wildfire around the world, killing thousands of vulnerable people. The powers that be, the scientists and the doctors do not understand it, cannot control it, and do not know how to make it go away. I am hoping that you do? Please tell me you do? You do, don't you?

To help me (and to save the kids from having a psycho-bitch mum) I have set some intentions for myself for this period of 'new normal'.

- *I am going to commit to my daily morning routine of meditating, praying, expressing gratitude, journaling, setting intention, and exercise. I believe that this will set me up for a great day and will help me to navigate this period as the best possible version of me.*

- *I am going to refresh the mindfulness training I completed a few years ago and practice being more in the moment with my kids.*

- *I am going to get out of my own way, dance with my inner critic, and do my bloody best to powerfully serve my amazing clients by being the very best yoga teacher and fitness instructor that I can be. I will repeat the mantra, 'This is not about me. This is not about me,' and learn to love, accept, and appreciate myself just the way I am – with zero justification required.*

Please help me.
All my love always,
MC xxx

For the past couple of weeks, I have felt like I am in some science fiction movie or something that you imagine happening in the future. The quote 'It's life, Jim, but not as we know it' keeps popping into mind.

I remember discussing as a child what we thought the world would be like in 2020. My classmates and I thought that we would all be flying about in spaceships with robots on hand attending to our every whim. We are not. We are being told to stay at home, avoid contact with our nearest and dearest, and try to avoid catching and spreading this deadly virus.

One movie which I have watched that had a massive impact on me for days and weeks afterwards was a film starring Will Smith called I Am Legend. The storyline is about a deadly man-made virus that spreads from person to person through physical contact.

When infected, the previously very nice person turned into a zombie-like psychopath whose sole purpose was to kill or infect as many other people as possible. The long and short of the movie was, from what I can recall, that the virus was created by a scientist who believed that she had created a vaccine for cancer. Millions of people took the vaccine and rather than it stopping them from getting cancer, it turned them into these zombie-like psychopaths instead. After watching that movie, I remember spending sleepless nights worrying about it, thinking how easily this could happen.

A contributory factor to this thinking of mine could have been due to the fact that I had just finished a course of medication to help me quit smoking. At the time, the medication I was taking was a relatively new drug, and the results were phenomenal: you literally just stopped smoking within two weeks of taking the drug, irrespective of how addicted you were to cigarettes. The side effects of taking it were, however, potentially pretty horrific – from really graphic nightmares to suicidal feelings. I experienced the side effects mildly through having the most vivid dreams for about ten days of me being on the drug.

I remember thinking after watching I Am Legend, 'I have just taken a new drug to stop me smoking – what if the long-term impact of taking this is something similar to what happened to those people in the film?' At the time, I put this type of thinking down to catastrophising.

Doesn't sound so unrealistic now, let me tell you – especially with all the conspiracy theories which are going around about how this new virus is manmade, for various reasons ranging from population control to helping to reduce global warming.

Let's rewind a bit, back to my sister on my doorstop and her not being able to come into my house and her not being able to envelop me in a massive big hug in the way that only she can. The kind of hug that feels a little bit like you are going to suffocate, and yet feels so comforting and reassuring at the same time. It feels as if my whole heart is breaking – I cannot breathe and tears spring to my eyes. I get this feeling that things are going to get a whole lotta weird, and I mean off-the-scale weird. Weird like we have all never experienced before in our lifetimes. I feel that I have absolutely no control over this situation – something that does not sit very well with me.

She senses my pain – she is feeling it too – and in that moment she makes a choice, a choice that I am more than happy with. She puts down her bag, strides over to me and envelops me in one of her massive hugs. And despite me being the big sister, the one who has placed an expectation on myself to look after her for all of eternity, I melt into the hug and sob, savouring every second of it. I do this because I know intuitively that I won't be receiving another hug like that for a long time.

Change is tough, especially when it is a change that we do not choose to make. When it feels like it's forced upon us. I completely accept that the only constant in life is change – I even use this when coaching clients, and I know that with change comes an opportunity for growth. When you speak to anyone who feels successful, they will tell you that to up-level they had to implement many changes along the road, and while sometimes these changes were made by them, very often they were made by others.

How well do we embrace change at the beginning, I wonder? How many people actually enjoy it when their world is turned upside down and inside out? I know I have never jumped with joy when God took my world and shook it up like a snow globe. Never once have I said 'Yippeee, I have been made redundant from my job! What an absolutely joyful day! What an opportunity!'

Does anyone?

Reflecting on this, I have noticed that I have been trying over the past week to make sense of these changes in the world. 'The New Norm' as it is being called. The social distancing rules which have been introduced along with all the other changes with regards to how we are to shop, work, exercise, and live. I realise that I have been embracing said changes in a couple of different ways. Neither approach has worked or served me or the people I have discussed said changes with. In fact, I am pretty sure that my approach has irritated a lot of folks – I know I feel irritated by it. The two approaches I have adopted are denial and false positivity.

Denying the Change

This has been my default mode most of the time up until now. It has been a combination of metaphorically closing my eyes, putting my hands over my ears, and singing 'la la la' while waiting for it all to go away. Sadly, this approach has not worked up until now and doesn't look likely to work going forward. The change is happening, and I need to open my eyes and ears, stop my awful singing, and do something more constructive instead.

Positive Pollyanna

Occasionally, over the last few weeks, I have gone super positive, off-the-scale positive, and seen the situation as a brilliant opportunity. An opportunity sent from God. A chance for us to all sit back, take stock, learn lessons, and then start again. No-one will be hurt, no-one will lose anything, and everyone will enjoy the process. If I was listening to me, on reflection, I would be irritated as hell and would be thinking, 'What actual planet does this person live on?' I am surprised I didn't receive a black eye during one of my Pollyanna rants.

So, what can we do during times when change is imposed on us and when so many things that we once had control over are now out of our control? How can we embrace and roll with them? My lesson, on reflection, is that we should do a couple of things. We should see the situation for what it is, not worse than it is and not better than it is.

We should also adhere to the beautiful Serenity Prayer, which has been used millions of times over for individuals who are on a journey of change on a massive scale.

> *God grant me the serenity*
> *to accept the things I cannot change;*
> *courage to change the things I can;*
> *and wisdom to know the difference.*

We should practice accepting and embracing change as best we can.

I have set an intention for myself to hold firmly on to my faith, my belief that God has a master plan which will eventually become clear. I will hold onto my faith. Not in some ultra-positive, everyone will come out of this alive and unscathed kind of way. More in an 'it is what it is' and we 'just have to get the head down and get through it' approach.

I have also chosen not to buy into any of the many catastrophising conspiracy theories that are going around, of which there are many.

These theories range from the belief that the government leaders of the world are trying to do a spot of population control like I previously mentioned. People are saying that they have released this virus onto the world to wipe out the old and the vulnerable – the people who are draining society financially and not putting anything back in. Another theory is that it is an attack on China by America, which has gone massively wrong.

One of the most interesting theories is that there is a real live Dr Evil like the one in the film Austin Powers at large who has threatened each of the leaders of the world that if they don't pay up (one million dollars mwah ha ha), he will unleash a deadly bug on the nation. This, it is believed by said conspiracy theorist, is the reason why Russia and India have had very few cases (they paid Dr Evil) and why Italy, Spain, and soon to be the UK have had so many cases and deaths (they didn't pay him).

I am tapping into my inner wisdom here and the way in which I am choosing to see it is that we, yes all of us, the collective – we have broken the world and have moved so far away from the basic rules of 'Love yourself, love your neighbour and love the world in which you live' that God has said 'Enough!' whilst pressing the reset button.

We are being given an opportunity to relearn certain lessons. I pray that we learn these lessons quickly and are able to return to 'normal' life soon. It is certainly my intention to learn my lessons as best and as quickly as I can. I do not want to live in a world where I cannot get cuddles from my loved ones for any longer than I have to.

There is so much that we cannot change at the moment, and we have to be ok about this. We have to accept and embrace this as opposed to resisting it.

I believe that we will have an opportunity over this period for us to make some personal changes. It would be great for us to be brave and bold in taking the first steps in making these changes, whilst remembering that Rome was not built in a day and that it is important to be gentle and kind to ourselves and others along the way.

Now that the world has turned upside down and inside out, I have been reminded that I have complete and utter trust and faith in God. I accept that everything will work out as it is meant to and that we are all being guided should we chose to tap into this. That said, I do have moments where this trust falters, and there have been times, especially in the last few weeks, where I have become really afraid and have felt like my head is going to explode. I have done my best to accept that this is a normal human experience, particularly during massive enforced change. I am learning to be ok with this and kinder to myself.

I have also realised that during this time where I am being asked to accept and embrace change, my morning rituals are a complete lifesaver for me – meditation, prayer, gratitude, journaling, intention setting, and exercise. Practising these things are helping to keep me sane and allowing me not to lose my shit (quite so much). Right now, I am grateful for the roof that is over my head, that my family is safe and well, that I have food and shelter and that I can feel and experience love. We tend to forget the basics during periods of enforced change. So long as we are blessed with the basics, nothing else matters.

It is important to note that some changes are harder to accept and embrace than others. In this new norm, where we are having to home-school our kids, I completely and utterly underestimated how hard a teacher worked. I mean, I always respected them, and I didn't ever moan about the 3.15 pm finishes and the long summer holidays. I did not appreciate, however, how much of a vocation teaching must be for the individuals who go into the profession. The teachers have added work to an online system for our children to do at home – it's amazing, and I am so grateful for this.

On the first day of home-schooling after schools were officially closed for an indefinite period of time, I made an intention during my morning ritual to run a tight ship. My plan was to get my ten-year-old twins, Maria and Charlotte, and fourteen-year-old man-child. Ciaran, out of bed and dressed for the usual time. I would 'motivate' them to do a bit of exercise, and then we would move straight onto lessons after a healthy breakfast.

This intention worked well on Day 1, and I am proud to say that I only lost my shit twice! Once with Ciaran who displayed the motivation level of a sloth on heroin and the other time with Maria, who must have painted her ears on as she did not listen to a word I said and when she did hear me, she argued with me about whatever I was trying to say. Charlotte was certainly shaping up to be home-school pupil of the year.

My intention worked on Day 1, but it did not work on Days 2, 3, 4, 5 or 6 (you get where I am going with this). Home-schooling was a massive upheaval for us all and so challenging. I am accepting the fact that I was not a good teacher to my kids during lockdown and embraced the wonderful people who have stepped up, during this period, as the amazing and generous human beings that they are. During home-schooling, the kids attended PT sessions with the amazing Body Coach Joe Wicks, art lessons by the very talented John Charles and science lessons by the Glasgow Science Centre – all FREE. These beautiful souls took the time to help our children's education, and for that, I am super grateful to them.

When we accept and embrace change, we really get the opportunity to notice how it brings out the very best in people. It warmed the cockles of my heart – and gives me peace for a bit during the day.

I have come to appreciate that when change occurs, we learn an awful lot about ourselves if we take the time to reflect and notice. I have noticed that I have not been as present with my kids as I believed that I was. During the home-schooling experience these past few days, in between the arguments and the strops, of course, we have laughed, we have connected, and I have really appreciated how amazing and clever my cherubs are. I sent a silent prayer up to God when Ciaran opened up his chemistry work and knew what to do – there wasn't a hope in hell's chance of him getting help from me.

Additionally, on a personal level, embracing and accepting change is taking a lot of digging deep and inner work. And I mean – A LOT! I have come to realise that I worry a lot more about what people think of me than I thought I did (more on this later).

Joanna, my sister, doorstop deliverer, the one with the brilliant cuddles is also my business partner. Together, we run a fitness company where we deliver a number of classes and one-to-one training sessions with a fantastic bunch of clients each and every week.

Well, we did until recently when we were told that we couldn't – that old Social Distancing rule again! We have followed suit with what the rest of the fitness world are doing and are now 'live streaming' online! The very thought of putting myself in front of a camera in full view of everyone is sending me so far out of my comfort zone that it is like I am on the moon and my comfort zone is still here on not-so-good old planet Earth. I am battling with thoughts ranging from 'Oh no, I am so fat, what will people think of me?' to 'I am not a good teacher!' It really has given my inner critic a fantastic opportunity to tap dance like that boy out of Riverdance all over my mind.

To overcome this, I am metaphorically giving myself a shake and utilising my go-to mantra of 'Be myself and be of service.' I am also bringing in the age-old thinking of 'If anyone is thinking bad of you, then they aren't your people.' I am having to work really hard to stop myself from going down this self-sabotaging rabbit hole as I fear that, if I do, my head will explode.

A great lesson to learn on any journey is to accept and embrace change. It certainly makes the road ahead that little bit smoother. I am praying that this lesson will stand me in good stead for the time ahead.

Questions for Journaling and Reflection

- When change occurs, what is my default way of responding to it? Do I resist it?

- What have been the biggest changes in my life that were inflicted upon me?

- What did I learn from these changes happening?

- How did I grow from these changes?

- In what ways can I accept and embrace change?

New Belief Statements for Accepting and Embracing Change

- Everyone, including me, is doing the very best they can.

- The Universe is a friendly place, providing everything I need.

- I deserve to be happy.

- I trust the Divine Guidance I receive.

- I speak my personal truth with love, passion, and commitment.

Lesson 2:
Adapting to Change

....

Spirit of the living God,
Fall afresh on me.
Melt me, mold me,
Fill me, use me.

Journal Entry

Dear God,

Today has been a challenging day in the Donnelly Boarding School for Magical Kids. I have come to the realisation that I am not cut out for being a school teacher. I am impatient, I find the technology difficult, I expect too much, and I cannot express myself in a calm and nurturing manner. I feel that all I have done all day is pick on the kids, shout at them and judge them. I need to be better to be the very best mum I can be to my kids.

I want to try better.

The lessons I have learnt today:

- *I could never, ever ever be a Teacher. God bless the teachers!*

- *YOGA is KING!*

- *The saying 'Feel the fear and do it anyway' is NOT just a cliché. It is something that should be taught to everyone from a very young age. HEY – home-school lesson idea for tomorrow alert.*

- *You CANNOT home-school and do your day job at the same time.*

- *I need to practice patience and mindfulness and lower my expectations from the kids.*

- *I never get a good night sleep after eating a whole tub of ice cream before bed. Why oh why did I say yes to Craig when he offered me that tub of salted caramel ice cream?*

My intentions going forward following learning these lessons:

- *Be a bit more relaxed about home-schooling and build in time for me to do my day job.*

- *Be on my yoga mat as much as I can to ground myself and forget about the rest of the world.*

- *DO NOT EAT ICE CREAM BEFORE BED. I sooooo need a good night's sleep tonight.*

- *Continue with my journaling, meditation, and gratitude diary.*

I also must keep reminding myself that this is a period of great adjustment for us all, and as with any change, it will take time. Please, God, help me to be a better home-schooling mum.

All my love always,
MC xxx

The Prime Minister of the UK, otherwise known as 'Your Pal Boris' by my daughter Charlotte, on account on me watching his briefings – A LOT – has just been on the TV. He has made an announcement that the UK is entering into a period of lock-down for at least three weeks. He came onto our screens live at 8.30 pm, suited and booted with his wild mop of blonde hair and told us that as a result of us not adhering to the 'social distancing' rules we were now required to stay indoors with only the people who live in our homes.

Ooops – I wondered if the Big Brother cam had caught Joanna and I cuddling earlier?

He stated that going forward we are only allowed to leave the house if and when we need to go to a food shop for supplies – he encouraged us to only go if it was an emergency and only to go on our own. We should not arrange to meet anyone at the shops, and if we did, the police had the power to break us up and issue us with a fine.

He further advised that we were allowed to go to a job which was deemed as essential to help fight the war against the Coronavirus. People from the emergency services and people who were part of the food supply chain were classed as essential. Otherwise, we had to work from home or be furloughed.

He granted permission for us to go outside to exercise or for a daily walk. It was stipulated, however, that this must be alone or with a member of our household and that we should never arrange to meet up with other people.

As I write this, I am experiencing another one of the frequent 'What the actual fuck, is this a bad dream?' moments which I am experiencing a lot of these days.

I breathe and say the mantra which seems to be on constant repeat at the moment, the mantra of 'Right now, I am ok, right now, I am ok.' This helps a bit and stops me from spiralling down the rabbit hole of 'what ifs'– looking for answers that just aren't there.

I have been working hard on accepting and embracing this change – a change which none of us has consciously asked for. Appreciating that with any change, there comes with it a set of new rules.

New ways of working and being.

I completely understand what we are being asked to do. I agree with what we are being asked to do. I completely appreciate the drain that this potentially could have on our National Health Service if we do not follow what we are being asked to do.

If more people get sick with this virus, then there won't be enough beds, oxygen, and ventilators in the hospitals. We are seeing this happening in other countries. The country most referred to at the moment is Italy. It was a sobering, heartbreaking sight watching video footage on the news last night of a fleet of army trucks driving slowly through a deserted Italian town.

Initially, I assumed that the trucks were filled with soldiers being deployed there to ensure that the Italian citizens were adhering to the lock-down regulations. When I asked my husband Craig for confirmation of this, I soon wished I hadn't. He explained that the trucks were filled with dead bodies – victims of the deadly disease – and because there wasn't enough space in the established morgues, the poor souls were being transported to make-shift morgues which had to be quickly set up around the various towns and cities.

My heart felt very, very heavy and sad at finding this out. I tried to blank it out, but the image of the fleet of army trucks keeps popping into my mind. I can only liken it to the image that I have in my mind following the aftermath of 9/11, an image we all have if we were around at the time – an event so tragic that it has made a permanent imprint on our hearts and minds, never to be erased. Those of us alive and old enough to remember all know and remember vividly where we were and what we were doing when those planes flew into the towers.

Boris's announcement of the lockdown rules came just after a period of feeling elated, having a sense of growth and of success experienced by both Joanna and me, as we had both just completed our very first live-streamed class within our online group. As previously intimated, this was something that we were both extremely nervous about and was triggering some personal self-limiting beliefs.

For a long time, probably too long a time on reflection, Joanna and I had been operating within our Comfort Zone – the place where we were ticking along nicely, safe and secure, not really challenged yet still relatively happy with our lot. Both of us had admitted to the other that we had that inner knowing that we had more to give, more to offer, more to receive if we just stepped up, pushed ourselves, and got comfortable with being uncomfortable.

If we moved into the Growth Zone.

This period of time has forced our hands, and we have had to move out of our Comfort Zones in order to keep our fitness business alive. We have had to move from a warm, cosy place into a place that is not as easy nor as pleasant. We have been required to step up and been asked to accept that in order to transition in the Growth Zone we might have to take a couple of detours into the Holy Shit Zone along the way.

The theory seems simple, but the practice can be a bit more challenging.

For those of you reading who are not familiar with all things related to social media, everyone, and I mean everyone, does 'live' video on their pages and stories these days. It is something that Joanna and I have resisted for a long time. We dabbled with it slightly in the past, and both hated every single second of said dabbling. We eventually just stopped dabbling, returning to the cosy safety of our comfort zone where we connected with our people through posting written text and images of motivational quotes on our social media platforms. We restricted our 'live' conversations to when we were actually face-to-face with clients.

As I previously mentioned, we are not allowed to be face-to-face with clients for now, as it is against the rules of the new norm. Yet, we desperately still want to teach our classes, which leaves us with one option. That being the putting on of our big girl pants and going live on the online group which we have set up.

The first classes we taught were a huge lesson in levelling up and adapting to change. I taught a yoga class at 6 pm, and Joanna taught a resistance class at 7 pm

What a lesson it was! I really had to dig deep before the class, get out of my own headspace, set my intention about showing up as the real me and being of service to my amazing clients.

'This is not about you, MC – REPEAT – this is not about you, MC!'

As 6 pm approached, I tried to go live in the group, and as always when moving out of your comfort zone, things went wrong. I experienced so many technical hitches. The first being that one of the girls who normally comes to my actual Monday yoga class called on our messenger group chat at 6 pm. When the rest of them saw that she was calling, they all answered the call, so I had six lovely yogis who were also new to this form of teaching asking me questions about what to do.

God love them; we are a technically challenged bunch, us yogis.

I explained to all their eager faces on the video chat that it would be a live video on the online group, not via the messenger group chat! See you on the other side of the screen, lovely yogis!

Onto the next challenge …

This came in the shape of sound when I went live in the group – and by the shape of sound, I mean there was no bloody sound!!

There I was happily chatting away, quite the thing, saying the usual things that I have heard anyone who goes live online say. You know, the 'I'll just give it a couple of minutes to see who is joining me,' and 'Hey Helen, great to have you join,' and 'Hi, Eileen, hope you have had a nice day,' followed by a bit of how my day had gone. I was getting into the swing of things, relaxing a bit when I saw a few messages pop up in the comments section.

'I can't hear you!'

'You are on mute.'

'Can you fix the sound please!'

AAARRRGGGHHHHH – disaster! I had absolutely no idea what to do! I kept talking, praying to God that a miracle would occur and the sound would miraculously come on without me having to do anything.

It didn't!!

The Big Man was obviously preoccupied with much more important stuff, and the lost sound on my first live was way, way down His priority list. It became apparent that I was expected to ride this one out apparently and fix it myself.

Exactly as we are meant to do when we are transitioning from the Comfort Zone into the Growth Zone.

With this realisation, I did what any self-respecting technophobe would do. I pressed every single button on my MacBook and, lo and behold, I was rewarded with a few love-hearts, some thumbs-up, and posts that I could be heard loud and clear! YAAAAYYYY!

Next challenge … teach the blooming class.

I moved over to my mat, took a deep breath, closed my eyes and………….

Entered the beautiful, blissful state of yoga zen flow, baby! I did not care a jot who was watching or what they were thinking. It was irrelevant whether the camera added ten pounds or if people judged because I couldn't stand on my head without a supporting wall for safety, or couldn't do the splits. It was just me, my mat, and my breath.

It was total and utter bliss……***Peace, perfect peace, is the gift of Christ our Lord.***

The class ended all too soon, and I came back into the room feeling calm, connected, and buzzing. I DID IT!! I was a go-live Queen!! Check me out! I am in the Growth Zone, baby – and I am loving it!

Joanna followed with an awesome resistance class, and the two of us celebrated our personal growth and world contribution with a phone call. Good times, people, good times.

We carried out a bit of self-reflection, and both agreed that moving out of our comfort zones is very scary, very scary indeed. The feeling that you are rewarded with when you do it, however, is incredible. We also noted that when you are made to move out of the comfort zone – when you have no other option than to do it, when there is no other feasible route available to you – then it is far less scary than staying in your comfort zone doing nothing and stagnating.

The Comfort Zone is a beautiful place, but nothing ever grows there.

Making the decision **not** to deliver our classes online and **not** connecting with our fitness family was never going to be an option for us. We owed it to them, and we owed it to ourselves to accept, embrace, and adapt to the change, growing and up-levelling as a result of this.

Following our experience in Rome, I believed that this was our time to up-level, that we were being guided, helped and shown the way as teaching online was what we were meant to do now, for now.

Resisting it was futile – it was happening.

As with all massive changes that we are being asked to accept, embrace, and adapt to, some things will click into place, practically effortlessly, whereas others will take that bit more time to get used to and embed. I soon realised early into lockdown that home-schooling was not going to be as easy a change to adapt to. In fact, home-schooling was going to be my nemesis during the lockdown period. An aspect of the new norm that I was really going to have to work hard at in the Growth Zone (and often the Holy Shit Zone) to enable me to learn and grow.

When examining how I adapt to any change in my life, I often remind myself of the *Forming, Storming, Norming and Performing* model developed by Bruce Tuckman. This model was developed to describe the formation of teams and the cycle of change that any team inevitably goes through. *Forming* is the early establishment phase – the creation of the team.

Storming is the phase where the shit hits the fan and what has been implemented looks like the absolute worst idea in the world. After this often extremely difficult phase, things then start to settle down and a period of normalising – *Norming* – ensues. People begin to start to understand each other and start to align with a common vision and purpose.

A successful team formation then generally moves into the *Performing* phase, which is awesome and great things happen.

During the first few weeks of lockdown, I can see now that we were working through this cycle, and when I wrote that entry in my journal, we were somewhere between the forming and storming stages. It is with some personal disappointment that I, hand on heart, can say that we never reached the performing stage during the home-schooling experience. What I can say, with a certain element of personal pride, is that I am pleased to report that no-one was murdered and that I only ran away once, breaking lockdown regulations.

It was not my finest hour – let's just leave it at that.

Being open, being willing to get comfortable with being uncomfortable and being patient with ourselves and others during the process, I believe, are vital components necessary for us to adapt to change.

Questions for Journaling and Reflection

- How well do you believe that you adapt to change?

- Journal a time in your life when you worked through the Forming, Storming, Norming, Performing cycle?

- What lessons did you learn from this?

- How would you approach change that was imposed on you in future?

- What do you do to celebrate you when you adapt to change?

New Belief Statements for Adapting to Change

- I trust that life will work out well for me.

- I am in the flow of life.

- I release the painful past and look forward to the good that awaits me.

- My life is abundant on all levels.

- I accept all painful lessons as positive opportunities to grow.

Lesson 3:
Belief and Beliefs

....

This little light of mine,
I'm gonna let it shine.
Let it shine, let it shine, let it shine.

<u>Journal Entry</u>

Dear God,

Today I started my training to become a Quantum Energy Coach. (How fancy does that sound?) I am so excited about what I am going to learn from Melanie and the rest of the people who are on the course. Thank you for bringing this into my life, and thank you for granting me this time to be able to do this.

Today's lecture was on how our beliefs are formed and hardwired in our mind. Talk about insight after insight after insight. It blew me away.

She spoke about how most of our conditioning takes place from the last trimester up until the age of around seven or eight years old. This is the period of time when we are like little sponges, soaking everything up.

It really got me thinking of the conditioning I received and the BS stories I have held onto for far too long.

I am making it my intention, here and now, to rid myself of these stories

*which have held me back for so long and to create new stories which I
know will make me happier, will make the people closest to me happier,
and will allow me to show up to the world and do your work.*

*Thank you for bringing QEC into my life. I am READY, BABY, I am
READY!!*

Please help me.
All my love always,
MC xxx

In one of the last physical church services that I attended prior
to lockdown, Fr Sebastien, our parish priest, delivered one of
his legendary post-Gospel homilies by telling us about a divine
intervention experience he recently had. He told us how he
was rushing about as he had to get to Edinburgh, where he
needed to deliver mass. He described how, when he jumped
into his car, he found that he couldn't see out of the front
windscreen, on account of a bird having done what birds do
best on windscreens.

Another Holy Shit moment!

'Random,' I thought – not the kind of thing that you expect to
hear from a man of God! However, if you knew Fr Sebastien,
you would understand.

He went on to tell us how, when he tried to wash the holy crap
from his windscreen, he found that he had no water left in his
washers. Raging and frustrated with himself, and a little bit
with God, he then rushed towards his house in order to get
water for the washers, which would allow him to wash said
poop from the windscreen.

Only, when he reached his house, he found that the alarm

system had malfunctioned, and he couldn't get in without the whole alarm system activating. This would then result in sending a signal to the police station. The knock-on effect was that he would be ridiculously behind schedule and wouldn't have a chance in hell's hope of getting to Edinburgh in time to deliver mass.

I was still sitting in the pew, wondering where in God's name he was going with all this. I most definitely would have had an open mouth and a furrowed brow, a very attractive look on my face.

He carried on regardless.

The malfunctioned alarm enraged and infuriated him further, and he quickly made a decision to go into the church to get some water from the small kitchen which was situated inside. He decided that he would fill up his window washers, drive to Edinburgh, deliver the service, then resolve the faulty alarm situation on his return. He had it all worked out and started to feel a bit better.

At this point, he admitted to us all that he was still a bit p-ed off with the Big Man for putting all these obstacles in his way. All he wanted to do was drive to Edinburgh, deliver the mass, and then return home for a cosy Sunday night on the sofa.

And this is where the homily started to get really interesting and had me on the edge of my seat, covered in goosebumps.

On entering the church, Fr Sebastien was met with a huge cloud of smoke. It had filled the whole building. He called the fire brigade, who came quickly, put the fire out and saved the church from a lot of damage.

They advised that it could have been a whole lot worse if Fr

Sebastien hadn't gone into the church when he did.

His belief was that, whilst he was frustrated at the time with all the obstacles that God was putting in his way, he was grateful to them now because the damage that would have happened to the church had he not went in for the water did not bear thinking about.

His belief was that God was guiding him and helping him and his church to be safe.

That is some seriously strong faith!

God bless that bird and its need to poo!

Our beliefs are what drive us in life; they motivate us, and they help us to make decisions.

However, they can also hold us back.

Our beliefs can serve us or hinder us – they are the backbone of every single thing that we do in life.

During lockdown, I was given the opportunity to notice and challenge the beliefs that I have accumulated over the course of my life. I have stopped, gone really deep, and spent a lot of time considering the belief that I have in God, myself, and about life in general.

I have taken the time to study the science of belief from experts in the fields of both personal development and neuroscience. I now have some answers to questions I have been curious about. Questions such as are our beliefs formed before we are born, in our mothers' womb or in a past life perhaps? Or are they something that we form as a result of our life circumstances and conditioning?

My findings are that one thing is for certain, and that is the beliefs that we hold determine our current life reality. What we believe, we receive.

Take Fr Sebastien, for example: his belief in God is so strong that he knows in his heart and soul that he is and always will be protected, guided, and loved.

In the situation he described in his homily - he was. His absolute belief in God manifests as a reality for him daily. He is always protected and guided towards his true path. Whatever decisions he makes in life, he trusts that he is loved and supported.

Our beliefs become our reality.

If I believe that I am good enough, I will be blessed with great opportunities, have better relationships and have a happy and fulfilled life. If I do not have this belief, then the opposite will be true.

If I believe that I am loved, I will go through life feeling and experiencing love, and this will allow me to have a happy and fulfilled life.

It sounds so simple, doesn't it? It is simple. However, it is not easy.

How are our beliefs created? On a conscious level, we create our beliefs based on our experience of our world. Certain studies confirm that this experience begins when in our mother's womb. Other studies state that we are all born with two beliefs – only two. The two beliefs are that we are good enough and that we are loved.

We are born into the world as shiny diamonds with the belief that our world is safe, that we are loved, that we are good enough, and that we have limitless potential.

Good times, good times indeed. How good was this period of our life? If only we could bloody well remember it. How amazing would that be?

As we grow from a baby into a toddler, then to a pre-schooler, onto a kid who goes to school, these two core beliefs can be manipulated and conditioned on a subconscious level, until we move into a conscious level of learning and understanding around the age of seven.

During the first seven years of our life, our beliefs about ourselves and the world are conditioned as a result of our external influences and environment. We are like little sponges absorbing everything that we see, hear and feel.

Research has proven that, generally, if a child is born into healthy circumstances, where they get to rock their baby world being naked, being adored, praised, and loved for the simplest little thing that they do – they have a far better opportunity and chance of taking the belief that they are good enough and that they are loved into adult life.

However, this is real life, and this does not happen very often. Sometime after we are born, sometimes sooner than later we experience a situation or encounter a challenge to these core beliefs, and we start to think that maybe we aren't so much of a freaking rock star after all.

We begin to become doubtful – and become aware of another voice in our head. This new voice is not very nice to us at all. In fact, it can be really horrible and cruel at times. Well, HELLO, Inner Critic.

Lockdown has given me the opportunity to reflect on these early years of my life and how my beliefs about myself and about my world were conditioned. It has been completely insightful and given me the opportunity to challenge certain beliefs which do not serve me or my world well.

My Childhood

I was the firstborn of my generation. The first child, the first grandchild, the first niece. I come from a BIG family – so there was a whole lot of love and confirmation of the fact that I was good enough and that I was loved. At that point in my life, I must have had the confidence of EPIC proportions, and my inner critic was away sunning herself on a beach somewhere, totally redundant.

A change happened, and when I was roughly three years old, I started the local playgroup. My mum thought it would be a good idea for me to socialise with other kids. Why, I do not know, given that I was the centre of everyone's world and really didn't need anyone else. I joke with Mum that it could also have been the fact that she had just given birth to my baby sister Gillian and having a couple of toddler-free hours was too good an opportunity to give up, especially as Gillian was one of those dream babies who slept all the time.

So, off I popped to playgroup.

In those days – my kids call them the Olden Days (how rude) – Health and Safety wasn't so big a deal, and in a lot of cases, it was non-existent. The playgroup I attended consisted of two large rooms.

The front room was for naps, snacks, singing, and reading. A spa retreat for children, if you like. Everything had a place, and on entering the room you felt instantly calm and nurtured.

It was so tranquil.

The back room, on the other hand, was absolute and utter carnage – you entered at your own peril. The noise levels were off the scale, and in the centre of the room, a large wooden, scary-looking climbing frame dominated. There was no soft-landing mat underneath; you took your chances going on that bad boy. Looking back, we must have all looked like a cage of monkeys from a zoo – dangling, screaming, and climbing around this wooden structure.

This was the 'playroom' and it had one rule and one rule only – anything goes here. Only the fittest, strongest, and loudest survived – unfortunately I wasn't any of these things.

I had a lot to learn!

It was my first week there when my very first limiting belief formed and hardwired itself as a neural pathway in my mind.

As I nervously ventured onto the climbing frame, I heard someone shout:

'What are you doing here? You are a Fenian! You should be at a Fenian playgroup!'

I looked over and realised that it was directed at me, and I had an inner knowing that the boy who shouted it was not trying befriend me. I had absolutely no idea what a Fenian was – I just knew in my little gut that it wasn't a compliment and that it was maybe something I should be ashamed of.

My little girl brain (whilst very intelligent for my age, might I point out) was not that advanced to process all this on a logical level. It was an internal feeling I experienced in my body – an off feeling, a feeling that I had never experienced before whilst in my happy little family bubble.

This was the first time in my life that I was called a Fenian – it was not the last. Each and every time I was called it or something similar in a derogatory way, I experienced the same off feeling, which I can now label as shame and which gave me a feeling of being less-than.

I now know through studying neuroscience that this ignited the creation of a conditioned belief in me that being a Catholic was something to be ashamed of. That, as a result of me being a Catholic, I didn't belong in certain groups and that I should never share or celebrate the fact that I was a Catholic. Until I brought awareness to this and did the inner work, whenever I heard the word Fenian, I was transported mentally back to the feelings I felt when the boy on the climbing frame called me it.

I now know that a Fenian is a term used for members of the Fenian Brotherhood and the Irish Republican Brotherhood and is now used as a derogatory term for Irish Catholics. The little boy who yelled it at me didn't even get my nationality right! Yet, still I took it on as truth and carried the feelings of shame for far too long.

This experience, along with many others during my childhood, awakened the inner critic in my brain. The niggling little voice that told me things that I now know just aren't true. Beliefs such as I wasn't good enough, that no one would love me, that I was too fat, that I was ugly, that I was stupid and all that other bullshit.

In that playgroup situation, being called a Fenian and understanding on an emotional level that this wasn't a compliment allowed my inner critic to start to whisper to me, 'You are not good enough,' 'You don't belong here,' 'No one likes you,' and 'You are different.'

So, what did I do at that moment when that first limiting belief came into my mind? Did I tell the teacher, ask my mum about it, ask the boy what he meant, retaliate in some way?

Hindsight tells me now that these would have been the correct things to do and that if I had, it might have dispelled the belief. If I had addressed it and talked about it, I could have dealt with it and eliminated it through processing, accepting, forgiving, releasing and moving on.

I was three or four years old, however, so I did what most kids in the '70s would do. I ignored it, internalised it and tried to wish it away!

This resulted in me having two very conflicting beliefs hardwired in my little girl brain. The first was that I was special and that I could be, do, and have anything I wanted.

The second was that I was different, no one liked me, and that I didn't belong.

This lit a torch under my subconscious mind to start a quest to prove both of these beliefs to be true. This is what our subconscious mind does very well: it looks and always finds evidence to validate our beliefs. Positive or negative.

All of this, in turn, started a rollercoaster of an emotional journey where sometimes I would feel on top of the world, completely and absolutely in flow with life, connected, in love and bossing my world, but at other times I would feel disjointed, unloved, alone, and not very good at anything.

It has taken a lot of years and a lot of inner work, therapy, and coaching to begin to put a halt to the rollercoaster and even still I occasionally catch myself jumping back on the rollercoaster, as a result of being triggered.

Over the years, I accumulated more beliefs about myself and the world. Some of them have served me well; others, not so much. I have positive beliefs such as I am intelligent, I am loved by God, and everything will work out ok if I trust and surrender.

I also have more limiting beliefs like I am not good enough and am going to be found out, no-one likes me, and I have to be strong and cannot show that I am feeling vulnerable and weak.

As you can imagine, there is a lot of conflict between these two sets of beliefs. There was a battle of beliefs going on in my brain to the point where I felt overwhelmed and frazzled.

Identifying how these beliefs were formed was a necessary part of my journey back to loving myself. I found it critically important not to apportion blame to the people who were part of the creation of my beliefs because they were simply operating as a result of their own conditioning and life experiences. They were just behaving, most of the time, in alignment with what they 'believed' to be true and right.

Just like I do not 'blame' my family for helping me to form the healthy beliefs – the belief that I am capable and can do anything I set my mind to – I do not blame the people who contributed to me believing that I am not good enough and that I do not belong. I take full responsibility for buying into both the healthy and the limiting beliefs that I have formed. They were created in my mind, after all.

I believe that on the journey back to loving ourselves as God intended, it is important to identify what our beliefs are and decide whether they are serving us well or not.

I also believe that part of our journey is to celebrate the

beliefs which do serve us well and to love, forgive, and release the rest of them with love.

During the period of lockdown, I was gifted the time and space to do a lot of studying and personal development. One such course was to study and become accredited as a Quantum Energy Coach with Dr Melanie Salmon. Using a combination of gestalt therapy, cardiac coherence, gratitude, and neuroscience, I have been able to replace the limiting conditioned beliefs in my mind and replace them with permanent better-serving beliefs. I have also been able to return to various traumas I have experienced during my life and remove the pain associated to them with forgiveness and release. No longer do I wince at the word Fenian, and no longer does hearing the word trigger feelings of shame in me.

It has been transformational both for me personally and also for the clients I am working with.

It is my belief (see what I did there) that God has guided me towards Quantum Energy Coaching to facilitate a return to loving myself and also to help others to do the same.

When we love ourselves, we have much more capacity for loving others.

<u>Questions for Journaling and Reflection</u>

- What beliefs do you have that serve you well?

- What beliefs do you have that do not serve you well?

- When was the last time a limiting belief was triggered for you? How did you react?

- What limiting beliefs do you need to love, forgive, and release?

<u>New Statements for Belief and Beliefs</u>

- I release all stress and trauma from my past.

- Every day in every way, I am getting better and better.

- I am confident and self-assured.

- I am good enough.

- I am loved.

Lesson 4:
Altered State

....

Walk with me, oh my Lord,
Through the darkest night and brightest day.
Be at my side, oh Lord.
Hold my hand and guide me on my way.

Journal Entry

Dear God,

I woke up this morning with a huge ball of anxiety in my stomach. You know that feeling that we all get sometimes. That feeling of impending doom. That something really bad is happening or about to happen, but you just don't know what it is or when it will happen. This normally happens when I have had too much booze, been partying too late (got to love a healthy dose of the fear to ruin your morning). No booze had passed my lips the previous evening, so it wasn't that.

I tried to work out what the cause of it was and established that it was a worry about money, about me becoming financially bankrupt and losing everything that I had worked so hard to achieve over the last ten years of being in business.

On top of that, I was having a seriously major attack of Imposter Syndrome. My inner critic was throwing a major tantrum and having a Best Negative Song Karaoke Contest in my head, singing 'U-G-L-Y, you ain't got no alibi,' along with 'Fatty fatty boom boom'.

The voice was telling me that I was too old, too fat, too wrinkly, not good enough, unskilled, not respected and not liked as a yoga teacher and a coach. It was telling me that I was a joke and that I should just give it all up and do the world a favour.

And if that wasn't enough (NO MORE, I HEAR YOU CRY), I had the realisation that I had become a comparison shopper and was comparing myself to my amazing legend of a sister and believed that I was falling way down in the rankings. All of this was bringing up a massive wave of feelings of jealousy in me.

A JOYFUL experience – not!!

Thankfully, as a result of taking some time to notice and take necessary action, I was able to alter my state, thank goodness.

I am praying that experience doesn't rear its head again anytime soon.

All my love always,
MC xxx

Who said that being self-aware was a good thing and was completely and utterly transformational? Certainly not me that particular day during lockdown, let me tell you.

After experiences like the one I had that morning, I often think about a tool I use with clients when they embark on a journey of self-discovery. It is aligned with the Conscious Competence Ladder which was developed by Noel Burch in the good old days of the 1970s.

I generally explain to my clients that the stages on any journey of growth or achievement generally follow a path which starts as being Blissfully Ignorant then enters the stage of being Rudely Awakened. From being Rudely Awakened, a choice is made to move onto Practice Makes Perfect, after which they will finally end up in the State of Flow stage. It explains how much conscious thought and effort is required from our brain in order to become aware and carry out a specific action or way of being.

Let me use learning to drive as an example. Before I had a desire to learn to drive, I was Blissfully Ignorant– I had no desire to drive whatsoever, I never thought about driving and the fact that I did not have the skills or awareness to do it never ever entered my radar. I was blissfully ignorant of the possibility of driving. It did not upset me, nor did it excite me. I was unaware.

This started to change when I was around thirteen or fourteen when I began to realise that there was a whole wide world outside of the little village where I was growing up, and over the next three years or so I developed a desire for freedom and a thirst for exploration. I realised that to fulfil these needs, I would have to find a way to do this. The conclusion I came to was that by being able to drive and by owning a car, I would be granted the gift of freedom and fulfil my desire to explore. The only problem was that I did not know how to drive, nor did I have a car. It was a Rude Awakening!

On the day of my seventeenth birthday, I was gifted with my very first driving lesson. What an experience that was – poor James, my very patient yet slightly crazy driving instructor. I moved into the Practice Makes Perfect zone. I made every mistake under the sun and stalled the car more times than I care to mention. I soon realised that I was not a skilled driver and would have to spend a lot of time in the Practice Makes Perfect zone.

By taking weekly lessons and by begging my mum and dad (well, my dad only the once, on account of us arguing the whole time) to take me out driving, I transitioned further into the Practice Makes Perfect Zone. I had been taught how to drive, I knew what to do, and I could drive with supervision to anywhere I wanted to go. I needed to drive 'with thought' during this period. I had to consciously tell myself to mirror, signal, manoeuvre, to feed the wheel, that the pedals were ABC (accelerator, brake, clutch), and remind myself to notice the brake point when doing a hill start. It was a constant conversation with myself and required total focus and my full attention.

After a few months of practice, it was time to sit my driving test.

I failed!!

My reason for failing was that a dog had decided it would be a good idea to lie down in the middle of St Paul's Drive in Armadale and refuse to move. This sent me into a panic – which escalated into a spiral of feeling nervous, uncertain, and incompetent, and I made so many mistakes. After dusting myself down and rebuilding my belief in myself, I passed the second time.

Freedom!

I was able to drive on my own and go wherever I wanted, on account of my Dad buying my Uncle's old Ford Cortina for £100 and giving it to me as a 'Congratulations on passing your test' gift. It was brilliant – I loved the freedom that having a car and being able to drive granted me and I drove ALL the time and everywhere. This allowed me, very quickly, to move into the State of Flow Zone, and soon I was driving without thinking consciously; it was effortless - the majority of the time.

I am sure, if you drive, you can relate. Anyone who has ever driven to work and then thought, 'How the Hell did I get here?' certainly will.

The same progression applies to the journey of self-awareness. In order for us all to become blissfully zen-like in that State of Flow the majority of the time, loving and accepting ourselves, radiating inner peace and happiness – we have to go through and sometimes return to the various stages.

When we realise that we are Blissfully Ignorant, that we are not fulfilling our true potential and living in a higher state of consciousness, connecting with the highest power of God – it begins to feel uncomfortable and unsettling. The light has been switched on, and you just know that there is no other way to go. You desire to move up the scale towards the achievement of State of Flow - living your true life in alignment with what you were put here to do.

There is no going back to becoming Blissfully Ignorant – sometimes I wish there was. I certainly did when I awoke that morning feeling anxious, unworthy, fearful, and jealous. If I had been in the Blissfully Ignorant Zone, I would have suppressed, denied, and pretended that the feelings weren't happening – for a while anyway!

I realised quickly that morning where I was headed, and I knew that I needed to take action to bring myself out of the rabbit hole, back from the brink, and I quickly delved into my mental well-being toolkit. I pulled out my first self-help tool – deep breathing to settle my body and mind. I tried it for a minute or so; however, I was too far down the rabbit hole for it to make any real, lasting impact.

I pulled the next tool out – a guided meditation – and tried that – still too far down the rabbit hole for to be able to fall into the zen-like state of blissful meditation.

Next tool – talking about how I am feeling to a trusted person. I turned to my husband Craig, and told him how I was feeling about my financial worries. He listened and was able to share that he was feeling his own fears – that the kids would get really sick from Covid-19 and there was not a single thing he could do about it.

Talking about both of our fears really helped as we could validate and invalidate each other's worries. In terms of my financial concerns, we could identify that we have enough savings to last us for at least a year, possibly two if we were really frugal with our spending.

With regards to our health, I helped Craig by reassuring him that we were doing lots to keep ourselves and the kids healthy. We were eating nutritious food; we were taking my superfood powder blend every day. We were exercising most days, and we were connecting as a family and having a good bit of fun. All of the things that help keep our immune system strong and healthy.

Talking about my fears and worries helped to shift the feeling of anxiousness a little bit. I realised, however, I needed something else to release the feelings completely. Again, I delved into my mental well-being toolkit and pulled out my Alter Your State Tool. I soon realised that the answer was that I needed to move into a new state. This felt completely the solution I needed to resolve how I was feeling.

During my time at the Unleash the Power Within event with Tony Robbins in 2019, one of the key take-aways I took from the event was that in order to lift our vibration, we need to look at our physiology, our language and our focus.

In the twenty minutes or so from awakening to remembering this tool, I became consciously aware that my language was focused on feeding my inner critic. My focus was projected onto the worst-case scenario and given that I was still lying in bed, my physiology was not resembling motivation and energy.

In noticing and bringing awareness to these three elements, I was able to call them out, and from this place, I could make an attempt to reframe and refocus. I could now begin to change my physiology and notice the impact it would have on my mental wellbeing.

Changing our physiology is about moving our body in such a way that a chemical reaction takes place. By moving our bodies in a certain way we release hormones and through the release of the hormone endorphin (the happy hormone) we start to shift from a state of feeling anger, depression, guilt, blame (whatever lower emotional vibration feeling you find yourself in) to an emotional vibration which will serve us much better.

It always works. Always.

I used it on numerous occasions during lockdown with Ciaran – my teenage son – particularly during the times when he was having a full-on teenage strop. I recall one such transformation in his vibration when I 'encouraged' him go outside to jump on the trampoline for five mins.

During one particularly joyful day of home-schooling, Ciaran was dragging himself around the house feeling like the whole world was against him, picking arguments with anyone who would take him on. He was not an amused boy. After a couple of hours of this, I 'encouraged' him go out onto the trampoline which we have in our back garden. He was even less amused at the prospect of this.

There he was standing on the trampoline outside, hands in his pockets, head down, a grumpy look on his normally handsome face – completely raging at me and the world. His brows were down, and he looked like he would quite easily have killed me at any moment. You could feel the dark cloud of teenage hormones hovering over his head. I stayed inside and watched him from the safety of behind the patio doors. I had locked them as a precautionary measure – just in case.

He then gave a little jump, then another, then another, then he went for a bigger jump, then bigger still……….and within thirty seconds the cloud lifted and in its place was a lightness, a happiness, and my easy-going, takes-the-world-as-it-comes boy had returned to us. His head was lifted, his shoulders were back, and he was smiling and laughing. He looked so happy.

We, as a family, were safe again – for a while anyway. Phew!!

By encouraging Ciaran to change his physiology, I was able to show him how easy it can be to change his mood. All it took was for him to move his body in such a way that he was able to trigger and release the feel-good hormones. Life always feels better when those good guys are floating around.

This was the main reason why I decided to go for a run that morning. I wanted those good guys to float around me. I wanted to alter my state. I knew that when I did, I would be giving myself the best possible chance of moving from my current state of high anxiety, which if I didn't address, would linger with me all day and stop me from showing up as my very best self. It would allow me to move into a state of high energy and happiness.

I coaxed myself out of bed and quickly got changed, trying my best to ignore the little voice that was trying to sabotage my mood, keeping me stuck by telling me not to bother going. Telling me that I needed a rest, to stay cosy in bed and that going for a run would be pointless as I would still feel anxious and low after it.

I went downstairs, filled my water bottle, hooked up my earphones and hit play on a podcast. I stepped outside and broke into a jog. Just like the shift I seen on Ciaran on the trampoline, I noticed that it was practically an instant transformation. Within a maximum of thirty seconds, I could feel the ball of anxiety starting to disperse, and the dark cloud over my head lift. In both of their places, I could sense the feelings of hope, joy, and love coming through. It was truly a magical experience, and for those of you reading this who have experienced the mental benefits that you get from doing some form of exercise, I am sure that you can relate. For those that haven't yet, I encourage you to try it.

Thank the Lord for exercise.

Within a couple of minutes, my mental clarity and focus had returned, the volume button on my inner critic had been turned down to mute, and I was starting to buzz with creativity – ideas were flowing to me, and I was excited about my future. I did not feel old, less-than, or unloved. I felt like a freaking rockstar!

The power of using the Alter Your State tool is incredible, and it is something that we have access to all the time – regardless of our current life situation or where we sit on the mental wellbeing scale. By noticing our language, where we are directing our focus, and how we are holding our body, we can change whatever needs to be changed. We have the power to make our day a great one.

We have control over our language, our focus, and our physiology, and even just the smallest change can make us feel better. With feeling that little bit better, we can take one more step up the emotional vibration scale, then another, then another, and before we know it, we have lifted our vibration and are feeling like we deserve to feel every single day.

Try these ideas next time you need to alter your state:

Language
Saying I CAN, describing the best-case scenario, looking in a mirror and giving yourself compliments, saying out loud ten things that you are grateful for.

Focus
Describing the best-case scenario, creating a vision board for success, reading stories of where people have succeeded against the odds.

Physiology
Lifting up your chest, keeping your focus straight ahead or slightly lifted, adopting a POWER pose, dancing, getting out a walk in the fresh air, running, doing star jumps.

Questions for Journaling and Reflection

- What language am I using? Do the words I am using have negative connotations? Is my language nurturing me? Could I start to use words that will serve me better?

- Where is my focus? Am I seeing the situation for what it is or worse than what it is? Is my focus on what can go wrong or what can go right? Do I accept responsibility for what I can control, or am I giving my power away? In what way could I shift my focus in a way that will serve me better?

- How am I holding my body? Is it closed or open? Where am I looking – forward, up or down? Are my shoulders drooped? Is my chest lifted? Am I walking slowly or with purpose? What can I do to change my physical body that will serve me better?

New Belief Statements for Altering Your State

- I love myself unconditionally.

- I take responsibility for my own wellbeing.

- I deserve to be healthy and full of vitality in every way.

- I experience harmony in mind, body and spirit.

- I allow the healing energy of love to flow through me now.

Lesson 5:
Your Shadow Self

....

I watch the sunrise lighting the sky,
Casting its shadows near.
And on this morning bright though it be,
I feel those shadows near me.
But you are always close to me
Following all my ways.
May I be always close to you
Following all your ways, Lord.

Journal Entry

Dear God,

Hello darkness, my old friend! I am comparing myself to others again, and I am feeling less-than. I am gossiping and judging and feeling like the worst person in the world for it. I am feeling fat, ugly, old-looking, and that no one really likes me. I think that they are only tolerating me because I have such amazing sisters. It has nothing to do with me; I am untalented, self-absorbed, unauthentic, and a terrible mum and wife. I feel completely disconnected from you. I keep thinking about all the shameful things I did in the past when I was jealous, angry and spiteful. Help!

Please, God, please help me to make peace with my shadow self and forgive the person that creeps up on me. Please allow me to release this side of me and experience the ME as I am at my core – loving, compassionate, fun, clever, beautiful, kind, a great mum, wife, daughter, sister, and friend.

*Please help me to step into the person I have worked so hard to become –
doing your work.*

Please.

*All my love always,
MC xxx*

What I did not share with Craig during my anxiety attack
during that first week in lockdown were the feelings of envy
and comparison that I was feeling towards my sister Joanna. I
did not even shine a light on them and admit them to myself
until a few weeks later.

I was too ashamed and too guilty to admit them.

Those thoughts and feelings, I believed, were too dark, and I
worried that he would judge me for them. You have got to
love a healthy dose of shame to keep you stuck, don't you? I
realised that these feelings and being in that energy of feeling
less-than were a major contributory factor to my low mood
and anxiety, but yet I could not speak about them to my
husband – I could not admit them to him. I could not vocalise
that I was a person who thought bad thoughts about someone
who I loved with all my heart. I could not admit that I was
comparing myself to my sister and best friend and feeling less-
than by comparison. I feared he would judge me as harshly as
I was judging myself and take away his love.

I feel truly and utterly blessed to be one of life's lucky people –
I actually get on with my family, I love hanging out with them,
and not a day goes by where we don't text, call, or physically
see each other. My mum and my sisters are my rocks; they

support, love and lift me up all the time. They encourage and keep me grounded in equal measures and, most times, they know when I am suffering from a healthy dose of the hopping hormones before even I do.

You can imagine my absolute dismay and disgust in myself when I feel anything other than love for them. It destroys and debilitates me mentally, and I feel guilt, shame, and anger at myself, and I seriously doubt whether I am a good person at my core.

This comparison and envy with my sister Joanna happened once before in my life – not when she was born as you might imagine. I remember that period of time with so much joy and happiness. I remember being so proud of her and wanting to show her off to all my friends. I thought she was the cutest baby that had ever been born – with the most infectious baby giggle. She was just adorable.

It happened just after we set up our fitness company – The West Lothian Zumba Sisters – and started team-teaching together. When we started teaching classes together, I felt completely and utterly in her shadow. She was this crazy-assed, highly skilled Zumba instructor, mesmerising to watch and completely entertaining with her pretend pouty lips and hips that did things that hips shouldn't be able to. She also had the most hilarious facial expressions.

I felt that I was not in the same league as her and spent most of the time when we were teaching together feeling less-than and inadequate, comparing myself and believing that no-one would really care if I was there or not as they were all only at the class to be taught by Joanna.

This was before I had done a lot of inner work and learned about the inner critic and how to validate a thought which was causing a feeling that does not serve you.

Back at that time, I dealt with those feelings in the only way I knew how to; I turned the situation around and blamed Joanna for making me feel that way. I made it her fault, and I genuinely thought that she was trying to upstage me and make me look stupid in front of everyone.

I withdrew from her and became huffy and argumentative when she asked me what was wrong. It caused a dark divide in the strong bond in our unit of four as my mum and Gillian tried to get involved to sort things out like the fixers we are.

It was not my finest life performance – believe me.

Deep in my heart, I knew that Joanna was simply doing her very best to be the very best teacher she could be to ensure that our business was a massive success. The conditioned beliefs I felt about myself, however, made me feel something completely different.

Joanna and I shortly after this switched to teaching on our own and the feelings I had diminished somewhat as I started to realise that people still came to my classes for me to teach them – my thought about them only coming because it was my sister teaching was proved to be invalid. I did not, at the time, address the fact that I was looking for external validation that I was good enough. I avoided that whole can of worms completely and got on with the job in hand.

And rather than dealing with what was really going on for me and learning the lesson, I stuck my thoughts and feelings away in a suppressed emotion box and slammed the lid tightly shut.

Fast forward to Lockdown 2020. Joanna and I have had to change how we are teaching our classes to serve our clients.

We are live streaming into an online group. We are kind of team-teaching again in the virtual space that is social media.

This has provided an opportunity for the lid of that box of thoughts, feelings, and limiting beliefs to fly open and rise to the surface of my being with a desperate need for me to learn the life lesson now.

I was massively triggered back then, and I was massively triggered again during lockdown – which highlighted to me that it was time to turn to the dark side.

It was time to face my shadows, shine a light on them, and heal.

My inner God voice said, 'Please, please learn the lesson, do the work, and I promise you that it will free you; you will remove a massive block, and you will become freer than you ever thought possible.'

'Ok,' I whispered. 'I am ready to learn the lesson.'

I intuitively realised that I could not do this alone. I would need support, help to keep me accountable. I also realised that I would need to be brave, be honest, and commit the necessary time and effort to bring acceptance and healing to this darker side of me.

It was also going to painful as hell – when I committed to doing the work, I did not realise how painful at times it was going to be. If I had, I might not have signed up for it, let me tell you.

I understand that when we commit to making a breakthrough, we cannot do it alone – God knows this – and once you commit, you are sent the support you need for the breakthrough. I was blessed to start on my shadow work journey during lockdown with the help of Craig, my sisters, coaches, and close friends.

Shadow work is based on Jungian psychology, where we identify with the darker side of our personalities (the part we often hide from others as we feel shame around it). It encourages us to embrace this darker side, accept it, and forgive it. Shadows present themselves when we have emotions such as anger, greed, envy, and selfishness.

Everyone has a shadow self, and by understanding what triggers the shadows, we can live with them and (eventually) celebrate them.

Shadow work often goes hand in hand with inner child work on the basis that our unmet needs as children play out in adult life as feelings of unworthiness, disappointment, jealousy, comparison, and lack.

I am very much still at the beginning of my shadow work journey despite all the personal development work I have completed over the last twenty years. I have a lot of layers to peel back. Admitting this demonstrates to me how far along this healing journey I have come. My default mode was that I could not and would not admit that I did not have it all together and know it all.

My belief was that if I did admit that I was a work in progress, I would not be credible, and people would judge me as 'less than'.

I now know that by admitting that you are not always strong, that you sometimes feel vulnerable, that you do not have it all together all the time and that you have shadows is a sign of strength and authenticity. The shadow work which I have been doing during lockdown has taught me this.

I am so thankful for the Quantum Energy Coaching sessions I have had during lockdown. These have centred around the shadow-self feelings I have about myself – my body, my looks, my ability or perceived lack of ability, my need to be noticed and loved, and how I often feel that I do not bring much to the party.

I have spoken about these shadows in great depth, and I have installed new belief statements to reprogramme my subconscious mind. I am, however, still a work in progress.

I have explored my feelings of inadequacy, jealousy, and comparison and admitting this felt so good to get it off my chest and admit it to someone and for them not to reject me. It also gave me a chance to have the insight that the one person I had to truly admit these feelings to was myself.

I realised that I had shut these dark thoughts and feelings away in a box and I have hidden away from them for too long, pretending that they weren't there.

My admission that I have a shadow self and bringing her to the surface with a commitment to take action was all that God needed as confirmation that I seriously wanted to address this issue and learn the lesson. Due to me doing this, due to me stepping up and saying that I wanted to be shown a way to heal, my inner wisdom started to show up and guide me on what will help.

The first thing my inner wisdom encouraged me to do has been transformational and has allowed me to start to make peace with my shadow self, to accept her for what she is and love her regardless of how badly she behaves.

The healing tool came in the form of journaling, which came as a surprise to me, as I have been a journaling junkie for a lot of years now. What was different was the structure of my journaling. I felt guided to organise my journaling in the following way to send love, light, and healing to my shadow self. This is how I now journal:

Step 1
I thank God for all my amazing achievements that day. These could be anything from washing my hair to keeping my cool with the kids to even taking the time to meditate.

Step 2
I list all compliments or positive feedback I received from others that day.

Step 3
I draw a large heart on a page of my journal, and inside the heart, I write all the thoughts, feelings, and emotions I experienced that day which I was not proud of – things like anger, comparison, jealousy, lack of love for myself, judgement, bitchiness, gossiping, etc. Sometimes I needed a very big heart shape.

Step 4
I write a letter to God asking for love to be shown to the whole of me, every part of me – light and dark – praying for acceptance and forgiveness for my shadow self, whilst recognising that it is showing up from a place of fear and a desire to try to protect me.

Step 5
I finish by praying for the release of anything
which does not serve me with love and light.

Within a few days of me practising this new journaling
structure, I started to notice that I was having less and less
shadow-self thoughts and emotions to put into the love heart
in my journal. I was feeling lighter, happier, and more in
alignment with what I know is my real self – the self that loves
me, loves my neighbour and loves the world. I have continued
to do this exercise most nights and, yes, there have been days
when the shadow self is more prominent than others. The act
of surrounding my shadow self with love, prayer, acceptance,
and release has started to ensure that the shadow feelings and
thoughts do not hang around as long.

I am very much at the start of this journey. It is my belief,
however, that the awareness of the shadow self is the final step
on our journey to true inner peace and freedom – true
connection to God. I also believe that we are only shown this
work when we have peeled back all the other layers and are
truly ready to heal.

Learning to love my shadow self has switched a light on in me,
and I am truly starting to feel so much happier with myself
and with my world.

I now believe that we should love all sides of us – light and
dark – and we will be free.

Questions for Journaling and Reflection

- What are your achievements so far?

- What have you done really well today?

- Where has your shadow self shown itself today?

- In what way can you show love to all sides of you?

New Belief Statements for Your Shadow Self

- I love all sides of me.

- I accept myself.

- I allow the healing energy of love to flow through me now.

- I love and accept myself as I am.

- I accept my imperfections as valuable opportunities to grow.

Lesson 6:
Body Love

....

You are altogether beautiful, my love;
There is no flaw in you.

Journal Entry - Love Letter to My Body

Dear Body,

I am sorry. I am sorry for not loving you as you deserve. You have been a best friend to me, and I have not treated you the same. You power me through every day, never complaining once. You put up with my constant pushing – the excessive exercise, the alcohol and also the drugs in my younger years.

I have never really appreciated how truly amazing and incredible you are. I have picked and pulled you apart, criticising your freckles, your ginger hair, your belly, your bum, your legs, your back, your metabolism, your hair that isn't straight, your droopy boobs – all of it. Through all of this, you have looked after me so well. You have never let me down – you have kept me strong, healthy, and vibrant. Thank you from the bottom of my heart.

I want you to know that it is my intention to love, celebrate, worship, and cherish you from this day forward. Please be gentle with me during this process as I have to undo a LOT of internal and external conditioning. Please work with me, show me the way.

Let's form the partnership that we should have all those years ago. Let's love each other, and let's be a Dream Team rocking our world. I love you, I am grateful for you, and I promise from this day forward that I will try my very best to give you the love, kindness, and respect you deserve.

All my love always,
MC xxx

Before the global pandemic (in the days where we could hug each other and congregate in large groups) I attended an event which was screening Embrace: The Documentary and was reminded of myself and my journey from a small girl into a woman of forty-five.

Embrace is about Taryn Brumfitt's mission to inspire the world to return to loving their bodies and embrace the uniqueness of them – a very worthy mission if you ask me.

In the documentary, she tells her story beautifully about how she went from hating her body to loving and accepting it. She encourages us all to love and accept our bodies, especially the parts which we feel are:

> *Wobbly*
> *Jiggly*
> *Stretchy*
> *Droopy*
> *Cellulite-y*

Tamryn now celebrates her body and the amazingness of it; she loves the fact that it has grown and fed two little humans and that it is strong, powerful, and healthy. She advocates having a balanced approach to fitness and nutrition and inspires woman and girls from all over the world to do the same.

I wholeheartedly agree, and I am also pretty sure this is what God wanted for us all. I do not believe that a God who created this beautiful, wonderful, breathtakingly stunning world would wake up on the day that he was designing the female and say, 'You know what, I can't really be bothered today. I know that it is on my to-do list to create the female form, but I really want to watch Netflix and relax (I wonder if there is a Netflix for God??) I will just rustle something together and then take the afternoon off. Who cares if it's not perfect? It'll be grand.'

I DO NOT THINK SO.

We are God's most precious creation. He devoted all of His energy, focus, and attention into designing and perfecting us to be the most beautiful, amazing, and wonderful things to ever be created. He took the time to make us all so unique and special in our own individual way.

Think about it – there is not one of us the same. Each of us is so rare and will never be repeated again.

And in return for all his efforts, what do most of us do on a daily basis to show our thanks and appreciation for this? We certainly do not jump for joy, expressing gratitude and love for ourselves, do we?

Personally, I have spent most of my life moaning, worrying, and hating many parts of my body. I have spent thousands upon thousands of pounds trying to enhance it, disguise it, change it, slim it, bulk it, and starve it. I have pushed it to its limits by intoxicating it, poisoning it, and training it excessively.

I can't remember a time when I completely loved and accepted my body and was grateful for it. Ever!

I know that I must have loved my body at one point, as I have a picture of me in a photo frame beside my bed – I was maybe about five or six years old. I had mad curly ginger hair, a face full of freckles, and the biggest grin on my face; my belly was out, my dress was pulled up showing my chubby wee legs on a climbing frame – I look completely carefree and loving life. Truly comfortable in my own skin and happy.

I look at this picture, and my heart fills with love and appreciation for this version of me. I can see that I feel beautiful, I am rocking my world, I have the light of life, and God's love is shining out of me.

This little me has not been impacted by the world too much and still believes that she can be, do, and have anything that she wants in life, and she knows that she is good enough and that she is capable. This little me, in that picture, doesn't care too much what anyone thinks of her and she lives completely and utterly in the moment. I love little me!

Something then happened to me on my journey, as it does to us all. The ray of inner confidence, love, and light that we were all born with becomes dimmed and we inadvertently, and through no fault of our own, move away from the story we were meant to tell ourselves. We buy into the story that other people, society, and life circumstances tell us. The story that we are not good enough, that we need to change, that we should not celebrate our bodies and that we cannot be, do or have whatever it is that we desire.

For me, it happened in primary school. Someone decided I was fat, and to be specific that I had a fat belly. Someone else decided that having ginger hair was undesirable and that having freckles as well as ginger hair was the absolute worst. These 'someones' thought it was their right to tell me this – and because they were my friends, I believed them.

BOOM – goodbye, happy and carefree little one. Hello, anxious and self-deprecating one.

For the record, I do not blame the people who told me these things. They didn't know any better – they were probably retelling a story that someone else had told them. It was not their fault. God knows, I have forced my judgement on what's acceptable and what's not onto other people over the years as a result of my own insecurities and conditioned beliefs.

The belief that I was fat and that I was uncool (on account of my chubby belly, hair colour, and all the freckles) was a belief that I bought into for more years than I care to mention – and even now I have to catch myself before heading down the rabbit hole.

Having these beliefs caused me to spend all my hard-earned pocket and birthday money on a face cream (that is most probably now banned as a result of all the chemicals contained in it). It promised to remove all the freckles on my face and body, leaving me with beautiful, unfreckled skin. I do have to say it kind of worked – and by using it every day I got so many black-heads and spots that you couldn't actually see my freckles. It also had the most awful smell, and no-one really came close enough to me to see whether I had freckles or not anyway. I got grounded for a week when my Mum found a tub of it in my room!

The belief that I was fat also took me down a dark road, and for a short time in high school, I had an eating disorder. I remember learning about bulimia and thinking, 'Yes, this is the answer to all my prayers!' (Seriously, MC?) 'I can eat what I want and then just puke it up, and I will be thin. Yippeee!' I also thought it would gain me popularity as all the 'cool' girls in my year at High School were doing it. I dabbled with it for a couple of months whilst at high school, and every time I had something to eat, I nipped off to the loo, stuck my fingers down my throat and hurled it all up.

Believe me, this is not to be recommended – take it from someone who has experienced and lived it. I did not lose any weight, nor did my body shape change. I did, however, lose a lot of marks in my test results on account of being unable to focus on my schoolwork and a lot of sleep as I was sooooo hungry all the time. I ended up hating my body even more, and I also lost a couple of good friends as I was too busy trying to fit in with the 'in' crowd.

On top of this, I coloured my hair as soon as my mum would allow it. The pain of that highlighting cap and metal hair hook still haunts me to this day! Talk about torture! Thank the Lord for foils – one of the greatest inventions known to mankind, I would say.

Over the years I have supported the diet industry by freely giving thousands upon thousands of my hard-earned cash to them just for the pleasure of being weighed on a set of scales in front of everyone in the room by one of their consultants every single week. I wouldn't dare calculate the monetary cost of each pound which I took off, only to put it back on again over the years. I have also tried every crazy-ass diet out there, feeding the belief that I was fat.

If all of the above isn't enough, I put myself at serious risk of death by undergoing a tummy tuck after the birth of my twin girls. I recall not even reading the list of hazards and things that could go wrong that the hospital made me sign prior to the operation – my lack of love for my body that that strong.

It is heart-breaking to think that I spent more time worrying about getting my body back into 'shape' after the birth of my son and my twin girls than I did thinking about how amazing my body was and how lucky I was to have been given the greatest gift of all. The gift of being a mum. The gift of being able to design, nurture, protect, feed and grow three little incredible humans to full term – until they were ready to give it a go on their own.

All of these limiting beliefs over the years created hardwired neural pathways in my mind that I was not good enough and basically unlovable.

When I reflect on what I have put my body and mind through over the years, I can see now how disrespectful I was to God. The poor guy must have been up there saying 'FFS, I sacrificed an entire Netflix boxset designing that ungrateful bee-atch – and this is how she repays me? Cheers, pal.'

After a lot of learning, therapy, self-help books, and inspirational role models, I am working towards returning to a place where I can celebrate, love and appreciate me. I am merging with that little girl who loves herself, cares not a jot what others think of her, is comfortable with her body and is grateful to God for making her so unique and special. Building a body-love toolkit has helped me with this.

My Body-Love Toolkit

Ditch the Sad Step

Standing on the scales on a far too regular basis was the very first thing to go in my journey towards loving and accepting my body. I have noticed during lockdown that when I do stand on the scales, I experience feelings which range from mild disappointment to very low mood for the rest of the day. There has been the occasional time where I did experience feelings of joy and excitement when the scales told me that I had dropped a pound or two. However, reflecting on this, that initial dopamine high hit to the brain was very short-lived.

Nowadays, I generally go with how I feel, and if I notice that I am starting to have negative thoughts about my body, I create time where I can work through what's really going on with me. It generally isn't anything to do with my body. I also eat intuitively these days and listen to what my body is needing. Sometimes it needs loads of fruit, vegetables, water, and other nutrient-dense healthy stuff whilst others it needs ice cream and pizza. I trust my body to know what it needs, and by releasing control of every single calorie and macronutrient that is allowed to enter my body, I release one more thing from my to-do list! Win-Win if you ask me.

Gratitude List

My journey back to loving my body started with writing a list of all the things that I have to be grateful for about my body. I set myself a challenge of writing five things every day that I loved (or even liked) about my body. In the beginning, it was really tough, and I was struggling with it. I dug deep and started with things like 'I am grateful for my heart that keeps me alive,' or even 'I am grateful for my toes.' By adopting a body gratitude attitude, my vibration lifted, and with the lifting of this vibration, the love for my body increased. I am now in a much better position and feel comfortable writing things like 'I am so grateful for my body – it is so beautiful' and meaning it – most of the time (more on this later).

Regular Exercise

The best quote I have ever heard on this subject is 'Exercise – not because you hate your body but because you love it.' I freaking love this. As someone who has had an unhealthy relationship with exercise in the past and used it as a means to further punish my body, I now see it as my ally. Exercise is my partner in crime, helping me to love my body even more. Regular exercise keeps me fit and strong physically and mentally. By moving most days, I know that I am enabling my body to live longer, and I am able to participate and contribute more fully to this life which we have been blessed with. My go-to exercise methods are running and yoga – I love the feeling in my body during and after a run. I love how strong, capable and in flow it feels during a yoga class (well, maybe with the exception of trying the splits, but that is a work in progress). Since lockdown, I have also started a love affair with weights and resistance training which, for me, feels like I now have the perfect balance in place. Finding something that my body loves to do, and doing it regularly is one of the best gifts and expressions of love that I have given my body. Again, more on this later.

Role Models

I became a big fan of Instagram during lockdown, and it has allowed me to find role models who are all about celebrating their bodies and who have a mission to inspire others to do the same. My favourites are Bryony Gordon, Chessie King and Taryn Brummfit. There are lots of them on social media – find them, follow them or even create your own body-love movement. The more of us who are open about our insecurities and willing to move to a place of love, the more we will inspire others. And that can only be a good thing

Vision Board

I created a vision board filled with pics of when I felt and looked my best. Creating this triggers feel-good emotions and looking at it when I am having one of those days when I just feel a bit 'bleugh' really lifts my vibration – and yes, despite all my efforts I still experience off days when I pick my body apart. That can just be put down to the human experience.

Body Shape and Colour Analysis

A few years ago, my friend trained as a personal stylist and body shape and colour analyst, and I volunteered to be her first client for a wardrobe edit. I am still surprised to this day that she didn't run for the hills, shaking and quivering, vowing never to style another human being again in her life. To put it into context, my wardrobe, at the time, consisted of black, black, black, grey, black, grey, and more black. It also had clothes that I had known longer than my husband of fifteen years (which were not vintage, might I add) and ranged from a UK size six to sixteen! You get the picture.

After a full eight-hour day, six black bags worth of clothes for the charity shop, a lot of tears and me having to be seen by an individual who was not my husband in an ever-so-sexy off-white thong and bra (which only had one underwire), we created my 'look'.

I am now fully committed to injecting colour into my life and to wearing clothes that actually fit me. I now tuck tops in to create a waist and highlight my great legs and boobs. I also spend a bit of time planning my outfits for events in advance, as opposed to doing a supermarket sweep one hour before I am meant to be going out. The whole experience was TRANSFORMATIONAL. I now know how to dress for my shape, which allows me to showcase the amazing body that I am blessed with. My confidence has soared in both a work and social context, and I LOVE dressing my body, which assists with LOVING my body.

Creating a toolkit that works for you and utilising it every day will really help you back to that place of body acceptance and love. You were created as a perfect, beautiful, special and unique being. Celebrate YOU!

<u>Questions for Journaling and Reflection</u>

- How do I view my body?

- What do I love about my body?

- What can I do today to celebrate my body?

- If I was to write a love letter to my body, what would I write?

<u>New Belief Statements for Body-love</u>

- I nurture myself in healthy and loving ways.

- I love and accept my body as it is, and as it changes.

- I see beauty in all parts of my body.

- I deserve to love my body.

- I am beautiful.

Lesson 7:
The Sacred Art of Non-judgment, Acceptance, and Forgiveness

··

Make me a channel of Your peace.
Where there is hatred, let me bring Your love.
Where there is injury, Your pardon, Lord.
And where there's doubt, true faith in You.

Journal Entry

Dear God,

What did I do well today?
- *I wrote over 1000 words of my book.*

- *I held space for a client to have true insights and breakthroughs.*

- *I connected deeply with my Mum, my sisters, and my friend Alison.*

- *I was a great mum and wife.*

- *I fuelled my body well.*

- *I handled the situation with Dusty and Benji with compassion and love.*

Where did my shadow self show up?
- *I was impatient with the kids this morning going to school.*

- *I was very money-orientated.*

I send love, gratitude and compassionate healing to my whole self. I love and accept myself for exactly who I am, trusting that I am being guided, being loved and cared for by you, guiding me to do good in this world.

All my love always,
MC xxx

The 3rd of April 2020 started out to be like any other lockdown day, nothing exciting or out of the ordinary. I woke up, did a short meditation on Insight Timer to bring in the Holy Spirit and got in and about my day. I made a huge pot of chicken broth – the stock of which I made from the roasted whole chicken which I had cooked the previous evening for dinner, along with the broth mix that I had actually remembered to put out to soak overnight before going to bed.

I felt like I was WINNING!

It was the last day of term before Easter, and I was feeling the relief of being able to ease off on the home-schooling of the kids (phew), allow them a bit of space to settle in to this new norm and dedicate time to growing and developing the online side of my business.

My phone pinged, and it was a message from my sister Gillian to Joanna and I asking us to celebrate how well we had coped so far with lockdown – we had not only become home-school teachers, we had also created an online wellness community where we were powerfully serving nearly 500 hundred people – helping them to keep mentally, emotionally and physically fit through this lockdown period (which didn't look like it was ending any time soon).

I reflected and gave myself a pat on the back and a high five thinking that this was the life lesson for today. Yaaaay, go me – I had not only survived, but I had also actually thrived in some ways. Lesson learnt! Woo hoo!

How wrong I was. There was a bigger, much more important lesson in the pipeline that day – ready and waiting for me to learn if I wanted to grow as a person.

The kids knocked off school around midday. We had the soup for lunch with minimum moaning about eating vegetables, and I taught a family yoga class online in the group.

It was shaping up to be a FRI-YAY!!

After teaching the class, I decided to take the kids and our Dusty Dog down to the local park for a walk. I sent off a message to Gillian and arranged an illegal meet up with her and her dog Mojo, as I could sense that Dusty was pining for his furry cousin and I was pining to see my occasionally furry sister and best friend.

We both agreed that we would adhere to the social distancing rules where we would all be more than two meters apart, with the exception of the dogs, who would spend most of their time together sniffing each other's bums. Why do dogs do that, I wonder??

It was so amazing seeing my sister, and we had a lovely walk around the park, laughing at silly things and pretending it was a normal day, joking about going up to the local beer garden to sit outside and have a wine. Gillian is by far the funniest person I know and always has me in stitches. It felt fantastic being with her. The dogs got off the lead and were loving the freedom of running about the park, chasing balls in between all the bum sniffing.

I thought to myself 'If Carlsberg did Fridays …'

As we were just about to leave the park, I saw a lady who regularly comes to my yoga class walking with a Lhasa Apso. Again, adhering to the social distance rules, I approached to say hello and see how she was doing during this challenging period of time.

After she fawned over Dusty Dog (who is very cute, even if I do say so myself) for a bit she encouraged me to let him off the lead to have a wee play with Benji, the Lhasa Apso she was walking for her old auntie. Thinking that it would be perfectly ok, I agreed and unhooked Dusty from his leash.

Within seconds of them getting their freedom, Benji and Dusty bolted off like a couple of greyhounds on speed up the park. Maria, my daughter, screamed, 'They are running away!' and my heart sank. The rational, default, always-expect-a-positive-outcome voice in my head said, 'It will be ok, they will come back'. It looked like they were going to when Benji stopped halfway up the park, as did Dusty 'Phew, it's ok' the voice said.

The voice was wrong.

Benji took off again at a rate of knots, followed closely by Dusty; they sprinted all the way to the top of the park, around the playground, over the little bridge which ran over the small stream and disappeared into a housing estate. Maria screamed again, Charlotte burst out crying, Ciaran set off like Usain Bolt, and Gillian became the commentator of the whole event which was unfolding before my eyes.

'Oh, they are running up the park, oh, they are over the bridge, oh, they are running towards the houses………'

What role did I play whilst all this was going on?

I FROZE.

As a Coach, I know a fair bit about how the brain works and how we all have a default response when a crisis occurs. These default go-to ways of dealing with a crisis can be categorised as Fight, Flight, Freeze and in some cases Faint. Thank the Lord that I did not faint.

I FROZE.

For a matter of what must have been a few seconds, it was as if time stood still and I went outside my body, went up into the sky and looked down at the situation which was occurring. I could see myself paralysed with fear, thinking that my darling puppy was a goner on account of the busy road that was at the end of the housing estate he had just run into. Especially as he had a predilection for trying to chase the wheels of moving vehicles – the faster the wheel, the better.

The voice outside of my body, looking down on the situation went into blame mode telling me that I, along with my yogi friend was to blame, that Craig was going to go mental, that the kids would never get over this, that I was a terrible dog owner and mother and that this was exactly what I deserved because I had broken the lockdown rules. The old Catholic guilt and the conditioned belief that I would be punished and sent to the 'burny' fire kicked in strongly.

How I wished I could have turned back time and not allowed Dusty off the lead.

The initial few seconds following Dusty running over the bridge into the housing estate towards an almost certain death were exactly how they portray it to be in movies – everything goes really, really slowly. Colours are heightened, sounds are louder, I became so aware of what was going on in my body and mind.

It was as if someone had pressed the slo-mo button on their iPhone, and an event that would normally take one second would take one minute. Towards the end of the slo-mo video, it then speeds up to double time as if to catch itself back up to real time.

Thankfully, I only froze for a few seconds despite it feeling like an hour, and I quickly moved into flight mode and tore off down the park after my son Ciaran. I remember thinking how he looked so powerful – his long legs striding and arms pumping, eating up the space between where we were standing and the end of the park. In two bounds, he circumvented the need to run around the playpark and cross the bridge by jumping the stream, and he easily ran up the hill which leads you to the path into the housing estate.

I was not as graceful, I can assure you. I must have looked like a woman possessed, oversized red dog-walking coat with the burst zip flailing and flapping out to the side (and not in the style of a superhero at all), gasping for breath, slipping into the stream and sliding up the banking of the hill. I remember thinking random thoughts like, 'I wished I hadn't washed and blow-dried my hair this morning, it will be a mess now,' and 'I am going to kill that wee bugger Dusty if I ever get my hands on him!' and 'This is total karma because you have arranged an illegal meet-up with your sister, you totally deserve this,' and 'Why the fuck did she say it was ok to let them off the lead?!' My Shadow Self, Inner Critic and Judging Self were rearing their heads in all their glory.

Embrace, Forgive, Embrace, Forgive.

I rounded the corner and saw two men walking their dogs. I gasped, 'Have you seen any dogs running this way?' to which they replied 'Yes, here is one coming back now,' probably adding 'Crazy-Mad-Frizzy-Haired-Lady' under their breath.

I rounded the corner, praying 'Please make it be Dusty, please make it be Dusty,' (enter my Shadow Selfish Self, one more time) and saw Dusty Dog running towards me, tongue hanging out, that smiling expression on his cute little face.

Thank You, God, I sent a silent prayer up.

He stopped and sat right in front of me as if he knew exactly what he had done with that sheepish look of 'I'm sorry, Mummy' in his eyes. I was filled with love and anger for him in equal measures. Maria came up with the lead and hooked him up, screaming 'Naughty dog, naughty dog!' while crying her little eyes out.

For a split second, I nearly relaxed thinking it was over until I remembered that Benji was still on the run. Ciaran, once he had seen that Dusty was safe had set off, again in the style of Usain to find Benji. I left Dusty with Maria and set off too.

A short way ahead, I saw Ciaran stop outside a house; he then walked into the house, and then I saw him backing away. I caught up, and he told me that Benji had bitten him when he tried to get him to come to him. My poor boy – he was the hero in all this and ended up being bitten by a dog. It wasn't fair.

After making sure Ciaran was ok, I asked him to go get Benji's leash from my friend and bring it back to me, and we would get him back to her safe and sound.

At this point, Benji was standing by a fence at the side of a house. A house that I later found out was his house. A house that he had the homing instinct to run back to, trying to feel safe from the puppy that was chasing him. I did not know this at the time, however, and my mission was to return Benji safely back to my friend.

I decided to go for the 'get him to trust me' approach and spoke to him softly, I offered him a dog treat from my pocket, which he took eagerly, and he then allowed me to pat him. Thinking I had gained his trust, I went to lift him, which at first he seemed ok with.

However, he was not … and again I was entered into a slo-mo, out-of-my-body-looking-in-on-myself experience.

What I can only describe as cartoon teeth appeared out of his cute, downturned Lhaso mouth. You know the cartoons where a dog goes to bite something, opens its mouth and out projects a set of nashers that has triple the number of teeth than is physically possible to have in said dog's mouth?

Benji opened his mouth, out of which three rows of teeth projected, and he then proceeded to sink them down into my hand.

I got that much of a fright that I couldn't even scream, 'OUCH – you little (beeeeeeeppp).'

I dropped him and jumped ten feet backwards as he sat there growling at me with his five million teeth on display. Again, I did what I seem to be doing best these days.

I FROZE.

I looked down at my hand; it was gushing with blood and starting to badly bruise. My first thought was 'Oh shit, I am going to have to go see a nurse to get a tetanus shot,' then 'There is no way I want to go to any form of medical centre at this moment in time given that everyone is working flat out helping people who have the virus. Also, I do not want to risk catching it.'

My friend arrived telling us that this was where Benji lived and that he had never run away like that before. She was in apology overdrive and was so sorry that this had happened and that she felt terrible that Benji had bit both Ciaran and me.

I told her that I was worried about having to go to a medical centre to get it seen to and perhaps get a tetanus jab and she explained that they do not give them anymore for dog bites. She didn't need to get one when Benji took a large chunk out of her hand a year ago.

'WHAT – cute wee Benji has previous? He has bitten before?'

BAM – this, I realised, was my lesson.

It would have been so easy to judge my friend for making the wrong decision, to condemn her and Benji for what happened and not to forgive her apology for Benji biting my son and me.

I could have become really angry, judged her and made her feel even worse than she currently did.

But what good would have come out of reacting like that? In what way would it have helped me to show up as a child of God showing love to myself, my neighbour, and the world?

My inner guide advised me to accept what happened without judgement and forgive the situation. It also asked me to reflect on my actions and forgive and accept myself too.

I remember that when I judge others, when I blame others for creating situations that have a detrimental impact on my happiness and wellbeing. Or even when I judge the actions of others that have no impact on my life in any shape or form – I am making a false assessment of a situation that I do not have the full information on.

I cannot even begin to know why or how a living being acts in a particular way because I do not have access to that person's mind and heart. I have not walked a mile in their shoes.

When we catch ourselves becoming consciously aware that we are judging another, it is beneficial to ask ourselves the question, 'What else can it be?' Asking ourselves this question allows us to explore the motivation behind a person's actions and gives us an opportunity to go really deep into it. It is often necessary to ask, 'What else can it be?' many times over to get to the core – the true reason behind the behaviour occurring – whilst also remaining open to the possibility that there might not be an answer or a reason for it at all.

Sometimes there is no why – and through having trust and faith in the master divine plan, we have to be ok with that. Sometimes we just aren't meant to know all the answers at this point in time.

I believe this to be true for all situations that happen in life, situations which devastate us like losing a loved one, losing a job, or becoming ill. Our default response is to judge that it is unfair that this happened, that we do not deserve it, that there is no God or that we have been deserted by him.

By asking 'What else can it be?' we open ourselves up to the possibility that there is perhaps another way of looking at the situation and that there is a lesson in it all – again being open to the fact that we will not receive the answer just now – trusting that it is all part of the plan and that the reasons will be revealed when we are meant to know.

By practising non-judgement of people and situations, including the judgement we make of our own actions, I believe that we grant ourselves an opportunity to move through them a whole lot quicker with less emotional attachment and hurt inflicted upon us. Furthermore, it allows up to move more quickly onto the second stage in the process – Acceptance.

Accepting that shit things often happen to good people for no other reason than 'it just does' is a life lesson in itself. It isn't about karma or reaping what we sow or even retribution for our mistakes and failings.

Sometimes shit things happen to good people – end of. This can be a very difficult lesson to accept and embrace at times. However, when we learn to embrace the lesson of acceptance, and I mean really embrace it, we are again blessed with the ability to move past the situation more quickly onto the final stage of Forgiveness.

Forgiveness is key to becoming truly at peace with yourself and the world, more connected to God. When we forgive ourselves and others for when we are not in alignment with love, we allow our hearts to expand and send out powerful vibrations to everyone and everything. Remembering that everyone is trying to do the very best that they can with the tools and teachings that they have accumulated over the course of their lives is so liberating, and it enables us to forgive the perceived wrongdoings of others very easily.

I repeat, everyone is doing the best that they can with the tools and teachings that they have accumulated over the course of their lives. Repeat this, make it your mantra for when things get tough, and you are faced with a challenging situation.

Everyone is trying to do the best they can with the tools and teachings that they have accumulated over the course of their lives.

In this instance, where we nearly lost our darling and slightly daft Dusty Dog and where Ciaran and I nearly lost a hand each (ok, slight exaggeration) from Cujo aka cute little Benji, I was granted an opportunity not to judge my friend nor myself for our actions.

I was able to accept that a situation happened for no other reason than it happened, and I was able to forgive myself for being silly enough to try to lift a dog that I knew had already bitten my son, forgive my friend for not having control of said dog, and said dog himself for biting me.

When we practice non-judgement, acceptance, and forgiveness, we also get to tap into a secret bonus prize, which is really useful in the instances where we royally screw up or make wrong decisions.

We get to witness the beautiful experience of not being judged or condemned, and being forgiven, which is beautiful to experience.

Because who here can hand-on-heart say that they have never done anything wrong?

Certainly not me!

Questions for Journaling and Reflection

- When was the last time I judged?

- How did it make me feel?

- What situations or people do I need to accept and forgive?

- When was the last time I accepted and forgave a person or situation? In what way did this free me?

New Belief Statements for Non-judgement, Acceptance, and Forgiveness

- I release the traumas of my past.

- I forgive (X) for (X).

- I forgive myself in the part I played.

- I release all emotions that do not serve me in my life.

- I refrain from judging others, accepting them as they are.

Lesson 8:
Creating Your Dream Team

....

Follow me, follow me, leave your home and family,
Leave your fishing nets and boats upon the shore.
Leave the seed that you have sown, leave the crops that you have grown,
leave the people you have known and follow me.

Journal Entry

Dear God,

I am so happy and grateful for my tribe. The people who 'get' me as I get them. The people who lift, inspire and support me every day and love me, warts and all. Thank you.

I am so aware how my tribe impacts my vibe and going forward it is my intention to hang out with people who are vibrating on the same or higher frequency as me – they are my people. They 'get' me, and they will help me to look at the world as a beautiful, magical place which I am blessed to be granted the opportunity to live on.

All my love always,
MC xxx

It is said that we feed off the energy of the five people we hang around with most. I must admit I never bought into this theory before. I guess that when a global pandemic hits, it allows you to reflect on these laws of the Universe more deeply and you are encouraged to accept them to be true.

Most Sundays during lockdown, I attended online mass within an online group. I mostly did this in my pj's, whilst still in bed, with a cup of coffee – it was bliss. One of the perks of lockdown. You did not have to get up early on a Sunday morning, get yourself dressed to attend mass.

The Gospel on Psalm Sunday really got me thinking about the whole issue of who we allow into our inner circle. As is always the case on Psalm Sunday, the Gospel was about the run-up to Jesus being crucified on the cross. Specifically, it spoke about the crowd he was hanging out with during that time –the twelve apostles.

It detailed the events which occurred in the run-up to his crucifixion, from Judas Iscariot betraying Jesus for some cold, hard cash to the last supper when he pretended that he had Jesus' back. It also spoke about how Jesus knew that Simon Peter would deny Him three times after Jesus had been arrested and how Simon Peter was appalled at the thought of this.

I thought to myself, 'Oh, I guess being two-faced isn't a new thing – it's actually as old as time itself.' I checked myself for this stinking thinking.

The Gospel then went on to tell how Jesus and his friends went to the Garden of Gethsemane to pray whilst he waited to be arrested. Jesus asked his friends to keep watch as he went off to a quiet spot to pray to God his Father to make what was about to happen to him go away.

On his return, he found a few of them asleep, and this is when he is noted as saying, 'The spirit is willing, yet the flesh is weak,' expressing his deepest disappointment in them that his apostles were unable to man up and look out for him in his darkest hour.

It made me reflect on what lessons I have learned during this period of time in lockdown in relation to the friendships and connections I have in my life.

I have noticed that the people I connect with have an impact on my mood, vibration, and attitude to life and that, if I expect too much from other people, then I am in danger of leaving myself wide open to be let down.

I have established an intention to always keep my standards high and show up as the best friend that I possibly can be. I should give fully to my friends without needing anything in return.

Additionally, I am embracing the fact that people are generally trying to do their best with the tools that they have and the teachings they have received about how to be a friend.

And finally, I have accepted that I just won't click with everyone, nor will everyone click with me – and that is ok.

During this period of lockdown, I have noticed that there are two camps of people.

In the first camp, there are people who are seeing this global pandemic and the shut-down of the world as a re-set, an opportunity to allow the world to heal, to allow us all to reflect and to choose again through learning what is truly important. They are no longer worshipping the false gods of money, status, and all things shiny, no longer forgetting that people have feelings and can be hurt as they get trampled by others trying to get to the top of the tree or win whatever race they are in. In this camp, the people appear to be very happy to have been given the opportunity to give up the hustle and bustle of the rat race, the control of having to have everything 'just right' and are content to sit at home doing a bit of home-improvement here and there, baking cakes and colouring in. They are also seeing this situation as an opportunity to better themselves through developing their skill-set and their minds. They are vibrating at the higher end of the scale. My sister Gillian is sitting firmly in this camp. She has completely embraced the slower pace of life and is loving having time at home with her dog and her partner, Dex. The vibration of happiness and inner peace is shining out of her.

In the second camp, the people are fearful and angry. They are raging at the politicians, the teachers, the world, and God (if they believe in Him at all). They cannot believe that they are being made to do this lockdown, they are finding it hard to stay in a house with their partners and children, they are spiralling because they cannot control what is going on anymore and are fearful that they are going to lose the shiny material trophies they have worked so hard to accumulate. These people are venting and expressing their anger and fear on social media and to anyone who will listen. They are vibrating on the lower end of the emotional scale. It is tragic and heartbreaking to watch, and I am praying that they will stop, accept, embrace and just be.

This has led me to reflect on who I have intuitively chosen to socially connect with during this lockdown period. Who I am 'hanging out' with in the virtual space and who I am allowing myself to be influenced by during this period of time.

The main people I am hanging out with are my husband, kids, my mum and sisters, and a couple of friends. I am so lucky and blessed to have a husband who makes the best of every situation in a calm and calculated manner, a family who are filled with positivity, gratitude and happiness and friends who see this as a brilliant opportunity to further serve the world. These are my people – the tribe which helps me to keep my vibe high as I do with them.

I am also allowing myself to be influenced by people who are very much in Camp One and are looking towards the future with hope and a belief that this pandemic will not have happened in vain.

I am restricting my social media scrolling to groups that I have set up, or groups which I know have the same values as me because I have learnt, sometimes the hard way, that when I go onto the mainstream feeds or even into other online groups then the vibe is a lot lower and this can contribute towards a dip in my mood if I stay there for too long.

On the occasions when I have ventured out of the house for either shopping or a walk I have bumped into people I know, people who I have soon realised after talking to them are living in Camp Two. They are bitching and griping about the unfairness of it all, how their kids are driving them mad, that they want to divorce their husbands, sack the government, and all they are doing is eating crap and drinking wine. In such instances, I have quickly employed a tool called The Bell Jar, which I was taught over twenty years ago on my very first personal development course.

A bell jar is a bell-shaped glass cover often used in laboratories to create a vacuum. When covered by a bell jar, an environment is created where the thing inside is protected or cut off from the outside world. By tapping into the power of the creative mind, and with a lot of practice, I have been able to visualise myself being encased in a large bell jar, creating a protective shield all around me.

The bell jar is invisible – no one else can see it and are therefore not offended when I put it on. For one, I would not like to offend the person who is spouting verbal diarrhoea all over me by saying, 'Wait a minute, buddy, you are killing my vibe here, just give me a sec until I pop on my bell jar to protect me from this negative outlook that you have about the world.' I suspect that they might want to hit me with a slap on account of them being in such a heightened state of negative emotions.

So there I am, with my bell jar on, listening to them giving it all 'what is wrong with the world' and 'boo hoo, my life sucks' and I notice that what they are saying is coming at me like a steam train – until it hits my bell jar, my supercharged protection shield, and bounces right off it and disperses into the ether.

It is a very powerful tool and one that I have used lots and lots and lots in both my personal and professional life over the last twenty years. It has served me very well and enabled me to keep my vibe high whilst powerfully serving the most negative clients – those who started off working with me with a glass-half-empty attitude about their lives.

The one thing about the bell jar that must be remembered, however, is that it has a shelf life of use. It only works for so long, and then the protective glass that is made of starts to become penetrable. When using this visualisation tool, I have found it very important to be mindful of this. It is my responsibility to remove myself from the exchange with love and grace for both myself and the situation and/or the person. I do not want either of us to be drained emotionally or physically.

During this lockdown period, I have noticed that I have intuitively hung out with my very own Dream Team, which has helped to keep my vibe high.

I would just like to point out, however, that this is different from having a friendship with a dear friend who is going through a tough time. In these instances, I am all in and there for them, shining my light, encouraging them through the dark tunnel they have found themselves in.

When someone is constantly vibrating in a place of misery and negativity, I believe that God expects us to try our hardest to do what we can to lift their vibe. The person has got to be willing and have a desire to change the way that they view the world, however. They have to meet you halfway.

Unfortunately, there are some people who are not ready to rise from the state of despair and are ok with thinking that the world is against them. I have realised, often the hard way, that this is actually ok, and it is the path they have chosen. I have also realised that I do not need to join them and that it is better for me to remove myself from their energy field with love, grace, and lack of judgement.

I have not walked a mile in their shoes, and I do not know what has happened to them to bring them to this place where seeing the world with a glass-half-empty attitude makes them feel safe and comfortable. I have no idea of the social conditioning and life experiences they have endured over the years. In instances such as these, I pop on my bell jar when in their company, wish them well, pray for them and send them love. And get the hell away from them before my bell jar loses its magical powers.

Finding your Dream Team is vitally important, not just during a global pandemic, but always.

Questions for Journaling and Reflection

- Who are the five people you hang around with most?

- List the five key characteristics of them?

- How do you feel when you are around each of these people?

- What insights/learnings/actions have you taken from reflecting on this?

New Belief Statements for Creating Your Dream Team

- I deserve to have full and rewarding relationships.

- I am able to be faithful to who I am in my relationships.

- It is ok for me to set boundaries and I do.

- I learn from my past relationships and create even better ones now.

- I am willing, ready and able to have powerful, intimate relationships.

Lesson 9:
Find Your Lobster

....

Bind us together, Lord, bind us together
With cords that cannot be broken.
Bind us together, Lord, bind us together, Lord,
Bind us together in love.

Journal Entry

Dear God,

Craig and I were out walking Dusty Dog tonight, and out of the blue he turned to me and said 'MC, I haven't said this to you this week, but I have been thinking about you a lot. I am so grateful and have so much respect for what you have done for our kids this week and always. You have done the absolute best you could trying to home-school them, and they are all thriving because of it.'

Talk about being blown away! I felt so noticed, so loved – that he totally got me, understood me and completely and utterly valued my contribution to our family. It has been one of the most special moments I experienced during the whole of lockdown.

Thank you, God, for my Craig-a-lar.

All my love always,
MC xxx

On the 30th of March 2020, 'Your Pal Boris' (as Charlotte is still referring to him) tested positive with Covid-19. He came onto our screens and advised the nation that he has had mild symptoms, and as a result of this, he was encouraged to take the test. He told us that the test came back a few hours later and told him what he most feared – that he had become infected with Coronavirus and as a result he would now have to self-isolate for fourteen days. 'Self-isolation' is another one of these new terms that we never really had to consider until this year.

Self-isolation means exactly what it says on the tin. Stay at home, preferably by yourself, until the incubation period is over.

In 'Your Pal Boris's case, on account of his fiancé being pregnant and falling within what is classed as a 'vulnerable group' (another new lockdown term), they cannot be together as it could be potentially fatal for her and her unborn child if she were to catch the virus.

So poor 'Your Pal Boris' has to stay all on his lonesome in the flat above Number 11 Downing Street until the incubation period is over.

When I heard this, I felt really sad, and it has opened up my mind to thinking of all the millions of people in the world who are having to do this whole self-isolation malarkey themselves. That is tough, tough going, and I am ashamed to admit that I hadn't really thought about them up until this point.

I am so bloody grateful for having my wee tribe under the one roof, sharing this strange and uncertain journey with me. I am especially thankful to my husband, Craig, who was and is absolutely incredible during this period of time. He has taken everything in his stride, been quietly capable, calm, and strong and has supported us all through a period of complete disruption to both our personal and professional lives.

Lockdown has taught me the importance of finding your lobster – and the importance of never settling for a relationship with anyone who does not meet your individual needs. I am so grateful to have found this with my husband, and for that, I thank God for bringing us together. It has also taught me that it is a two-way thing and that I am responsible for fulfilling his needs and wants too.

Before I begin, it might be worthwhile to explain the 'Find Your Lobster' reference. I first heard this during an episode of Friends way back in the day when I had time to sit for hours on end watching boxsets – which were, in fact, VHS videotapes in an actual box – God I am old!

The particular Lobster episode was the one where Pheobe (the blonde one) tells Ross (the dinosaur one) that Rachel (the lucky one on account of dating Brad Pitt) is 'his Lobster'. When questioned, she explains that when lobsters mate, it's for life, and you can actually see old lobsters walking around claw-in-claw as happily in lobster-love as the day they met.

My Craigy Boy is my Lobster.

In my late twenties, I worked in Human Resources. The one aspect of the role that I loved was recruitment, specifically creating job advertisements which would be placed in the newspaper. The more creative I could be with an advert, the more I vibrated on a really high frequency. It was a passion of mine. I got so excited to see an advert which I had created printed in The Scotsman or The West Lothian Courier. It made me feel very proud of myself.

This was in the olden days, of course, before everything moved to online.

At this particular time in my life, I was single and had been for what felt like forever. I really wanted to meet someone special, settle down with them and live happily ever after. Disney has a LOT to answer for. Every time I thought I had met someone decent, it quickly resulted in us not being a match – with varying degrees of tears and drama, mostly on my part.

I was beginning to despair and was starting to seriously consider the option of becoming a nun. I suppose if I had, I would have been the proud owner of the red invite that our giggling nun friends were in possession of to gain 'legitimate' entry into the Vatican on that special day in Rome.

I would also have had far less body image issues, on account of the 'hides a multitude of sins' habits that they get to wear.

However, rather than pledging my life to God in that way, I decided to create an advert like the job adverts I loved to design, although this time it would be for me to recruit my lobster. I didn't post it in any 'Lonely Hearts' column or stick in any shop windows (again, before online dating). I simply created the advert and sent it up to God with a prayer that it would be answered. It was. Shortly afterwards, I was blessed with meeting Craig and found my happily (most of the time) ever after.

I still have a copy of the advert, and to this day, it blows me away every time I look at it. The advert detailed all the things I was looking for from the relationship with my significant other. It was in the form of an acronym which spelt out the words FIT BLOKE. Each letter was the first letter of what I wanted from the relationship.

To this day, this still holds true, and these are the same things that I want from the relationship I have with my soulmate. They are also the things that I want to bring to the relationship too.

F – Fun and Excitement
I – Interested
T – Trust and Honesty

B – Bedtime adventures
L – Love
O – One Agenda
K – Kindness and Compassion
E – Equality

Fun and Excitement

When you have a young family, finding the time just for the two of you to go out and have fun can often be nigh on impossible. Craig and I experienced this at the beginning of our relationship until we realised that it had to be made a priority. When we made time for just the two of us to have fun and adventures as a couple, not only did our relationship benefit, we also became positive role models for our kids when they saw their parents still loving life and doing things together. Well, until Maria suggested that maybe we were doing it a bit TOO OFTEN.

Craig and I have been lucky enough to share so many exciting adventures, from holidays in Ibiza and Vegas, to music festivals, to completing a triathlon. Doing exciting things as a couple keeps it fresh and reminds us why we fell in love with each other in the first place.

We also make it a practice to find fun and excitement in the mundane, the ordinary aspects of daily life. This is vitally important to keep the magic alive.

Interested

Being interested in the other person is vital for any relationship to succeed. I always find that Craig and I are more connected when we take the time to find out how the other person is doing. What is going on for us? Lockdown was brilliant for this as it has given us both the opportunity to work from home, which means we are not so much ships that pass in the night like we were prior to lockdown. We chat lots whilst out on walks, and I have been reminded how interested I am in hearing what Craig has to say – he has great ideas and opinions.

Trust and Honesty

A relationship without trust is a tough relationship to sustain, and in our early years, I did struggle with the whole trust thing. This was on account of how I allowed myself to be treated during previous relationships and my own limiting beliefs on my worthiness of being able to have the relationship of my wildest dreams with my soulmate.

Through becoming honest with myself, honest with Craig and doing a LOT of work on myself, I am now in a position where I am able to trust him unconditionally – the majority of the time. The times when I fall into old habits and patterns are triggers for me to go deeper and do the inner work required of me. It is always about me, never about Craig. I know this now.

I believe that honesty is fundamental to the success of any relationship. Both parties need to be brave enough to be respectfully honest with each other. By respectfully, it is about sharing what isn't working without blame, accusation or shaming them. In the beginning, there was a lot of brushing under the carpet with Craig and I and avoiding the humungous elephant in the room.

But here is the thing with all the ignoring and avoiding – it NEVER goes away, and you get presented with the lesson time and time and time again until you bloody well learn it. Through being brave and through setting a powerful intention before having a difficult conversation Craig and I have been able to become truly honest about how we feel, and as a result of doing this, we have improved the quality of our relationship one million per cent.

Bedtime Adventures

Yep, I am going to write about SEX, people. Cover your eyes, Mum! Keeping the sexual magic alive is vital for the success of a relationship which has been entered into on the premise that both parties have a desire to connect physically.

If you have chosen to be in a sexual relationship and have never experienced magical bedroom adventures, then take responsibility for that and bring your sexual needs and desires to the bedroom, seeking help if necessary.

If you are an individual with a desire to connect physically – you deserve to connect and have toe-curling moments in abundance.

Loving

A loving relationship is based on a number of different factors. One such factor is patience. By practising patience with a partner (I know it's a challenge at times), we can step away from our agenda and see things from another person's perspective, which allows us to grow as individuals and realise that not everything needs to be done yesterday. Craig has allowed me to practice patience so much over the years with his methodical approach to life and for that I thank him – but

PLEASE PLEASE PLEASE paint the upstairs bathroom sometime this century!

Another key component is respect, and by this I mean a mutual admiration and recognition for each other. A belief in your heart that each person in the relationship is doing the very best that they can with the tools that they have at their current disposal.

Compromise is key for any loving relationship to work. By compromise, I do not mean you should sacrifice the BIG goals which you want to achieve in life, and I certainly do not mean your partner should ever expect you to give up working on your hearts' desire. I have found over the years, however, to be mindful of Craig's goals too and that sometimes the family agenda should be worked on before my agenda. And I am completely ok with that.

One Agenda

It is invaluable to ensure success in a relationship to jointly complete a goal-setting exercise. Craig and I do this a couple of times each year. The session consists of discussing and creating Couple Goals, Family Goals, Personal Goals, Fun Goals, Growth Goals and Material Goals.

By completing this exercise as a couple both parties will know what each other wants from life, what is truly important, and from this place of clarity, you will be able to prioritise jointly where the focus of attention should be placed.

We did have to re-evaluate the goals we set in January 2020, for obvious reasons.

Kindness and Compassion

This is key. In any relationship, both parties are going to royally muck it up. Often BIG TIME. It is important to show kindness and compassion when this happens. Unless it is repeated poor behaviour. This is unacceptable and should not be tolerated!

However, in order for a relationship to work, it is so important to display kindness and compassion to our partner and remember that they are operating from the conditioning that they have experienced in the past. By forgiving them, being kind and showing compassion, we can create a relationship built on love, joy, and connection.

Being kind and compassionate is not about being weak and giving in; it is a sign of being brave and strong, giving the other person permission to be the same.

Equality

Equality in a relationship means different things to different couples, and as long as both parties feel satisfied with the effort which the other person is putting into the relationship, then that is fine and dandy. Where disharmony in relationships can occur, is where one party feels that there is an imbalance in effort. In this instance, it is an easy option to let it fester. An easy option until it becomes a melting pot of resentment – and then they blow. I know, I have been there. With a lot of self-reflection and honest conversations I am happy to report that in this house, it is generally a 50/50 split between everything from chores to financial contribution to allowing the other person 'me time'.

Having a relationship is amazing and incredible. It is also bloody tough. Sustaining a relationship where you are both happy and fulfilled is a massive achievement and should be celebrated together.

I am celebrating the fact that I still love Craig despite the fact that he farts in bed, gets food in his beard and tells cringy jokes. Craig celebrates that he still loves me despite the fact that I fart in bed, talk with my mouth full of food and take life too seriously a lot of the time. As a couple we are celebrating that we have managed to grow three incredible humans that we love to the ends of this earth despite the fact that they fart in bed, fight with us about eating vegetables and moan about tidying their rooms. Celebrate it all. The good, the average, the awful. You get the idea.

I need to remember this last point when he farts in bed, tells a cringy joke and gets food in his beard!

<u>Questions for Journaling and Reflection</u>

- What am I looking for in a relationship?

- What would a loving, happy relationship look like for me?

- What do I need to let go of from previous relationships that will not serve me going forward?

- What responsibility do I need to take for having a happy, loving relationship?

<u>New Belief Statements for Finding Your Lobster</u>

- I allow myself to be vulnerable and sensitive in a relationship.

- I am able to speak my truth.

- It is easy for me to receive love.

- I allow myself to open my heart and surrender fully to a relationship.

- I am willing to risk loving and being loved.

Lesson 10:
Thought-based Realities

....

Love is flowing like a river,
Flowing out through you and me.
Love is flowing like a river,
Setting all the captives free.

Journal Entry

Dear God,

I feel like I have been transported back in time. Judging by what I have been seeing and hearing from others, they have too. It is like we have all been transported back to a time when things were simpler, easier and more connected. In my heart, I feel that this is a good thing.

Today, I made a picnic, and we all went down 'The Glen'. It was so beautiful; fourteen years I have lived in Armadale and have never taken the time to appreciate how lovely it is and what is right under my nose. The kids paddled in the river, we played catch with a tennis ball, and on the way back we talked about our family tree. If Carlberg did Fridays – this would be one of them.

Thank you.

All my love always,
MC xxx

These are just some of the things which I experienced during lockdown.

Family units are going out for lovely walks.

Every time I am out with my tribe, I see other tribes out walking. We smile and say hello to each other and genuinely notice each other. It is very special.

What is also lovely to see is that the tribes are all interacting with each other, most of the time. Teenagers are walking with their heads looking forward as opposed to down into a mobile phone (which makes my heart sing with joy as I often get the fear for the development of their spines). Adults are talking to each other again, which is lovely.

Craig and I have had some of the best chats of our married life together whilst out on our lockdown walks.

People are baking, knitting and crafting.

My mum delivered a doorstop delivery of Irish soda bread to me yesterday. She had baked it herself. It reminded me so much of visiting my Nana's when I was young. She always baked her own bread, and you always got a heavily buttered slice along with the tiniest glass of lemonade to wash it down.

All over social media, I am seeing people knitting, crafting, starting (and finishing) upcycling projects which are amazing and fill them with so much joy, fulfilment, and contentment.

People are taking care of their homes.

There are a hell of a lot of painted fences everywhere, including ours, which the girls painted bright and colourful in honour of the efforts of the NHS. The companies who manufacture outdoor paint will be delighted with this turn of events, I would imagine. People have invested in painting bedrooms, with the masking taped triangles of colour being very on-trend this lockdown, and gardens have never looked as pretty.

People are taking the time to get to know and talk to their neighbours.

Like really taking the time to find out how they are (from an appropriate social distance, obviously). We are finding out if our neighbours need anything, we are listening, fully and presently, as opposed to a quick 'Hiya, how are you doing?' before jumping in the car and driving off at breakneck speak to do the next thing on our list.

Old school board games have been dug out.

I see families all over social media engaging in a good old game of Scrabble, Trivial Pursuit, and even the retro Hungry Hippos on one occasion.

I would like to note that this has never happened in our house because the Donnelly's playing board games never ever ends well. And I mean NEVER!! We can almost manage a game of Scabby Queen without us all falling out.

No one is booking flights or caring about jetting off to foreign countries for holidays.

Which obviously will have an impact on holiday companies and the airline industry, which is awful. I would never want to see any company going out of business.

It is, however, making us more interested in our own country and appreciating the absolute beauty which we have on our doorstep. We have lived in Armadale for fourteen years, and I have never taken the time to explore it. On that lovely, sunny day in my journal entry, I packed a picnic, and we all as a family went down to the river that runs along the bottom of the town. We found a beautiful grassy spot where we sat and ate our lunch. Afterwards, the kids had a little paddle in the river, and we entertained ourselves by playing catch with a tennis ball.

It was so much fun (which was confirmed by the kids, too) and reminded me of my childhood when all you needed was a sunny day, a friend, and access to water to make a memory which would last a lifetime.

Further afield, about seven miles from our home, we found a beautiful lagoon, which we did not know existed, where we could all go for an open water swim one gorgeously sunny afternoon. It was heavenly and started my passion for open-water swimming – something I would never have made the time to do were it not for lockdown.

We are taking the time to be present with our children.

I have found that I have never spoken so much to my kids as I have during lockdown. It turns out they love hearing stories of the 'olden days' (I have to let this one pass) and what I got up to when I was younger. The fun I had, the trouble I got into and what life was like for me growing up.

Remembering and sharing these stories has opened up a part of my brain that I had forgotten about. We often only remember the not-so-good times, the memories that create the limiting beliefs in you now.

Exploring the good times that happened in my past and having a laugh about them has been a major insight for me, the insight being that I have, in fact, lived an incredibly happy and fulfilled life. I have experienced so much. I have bloody well lived. I have also been reminded that I am so much more than the limiting beliefs that can sometimes hold me back.

By taking this time to be fully present, I am being reminded of how awesome my kids are and how it is an honour to be blessed with the job of growing these incredible little humans.

Now, don't get me wrong – they do still drive me mental A LOT of the time. Like the time during lockdown when I asked Ciaran to watch over the pot of soup that I had put on whilst I went out a run. To cut a long story short, we had no soup for lunch that day – and I needed a new pot!!

In the main, however, they are funny, sassy, kind, intelligent, great company and a pleasure to get to know. Something that I had lost sight off when I was on my BC hamster wheel.

No-one is bothered about what car anyone drives, what job anyone has or how much money is in the bank.

All that superficial shit just does not matter anymore. It never has, and it is refreshing to see that people are realising this. When the world starts turning again, I truly hope that we all remember this.

We are shopping local and supporting our neighbours and friends.

We have to be really conscious of when we go out of our home and that the times when we do go out should only be for an 'essential' reason. As a result of this, we are doing a lot of our shopping whilst out on our walks. This means that we are stopping by local butchers, fruit shops and general all-purpose shops to get what we need, as opposed to venturing too far away from our homes to go to the big supermarkets.

I believe this has also been a conscious decision to help keep local entrepreneurs afloat during this worrying time. We want to help the people we know through this difficult economic time, to ensure that they stay the distance and are still able to do what they do best after it is all over.

In terms of the businesses I am involved with – my superfood company, the fitness company, and the salon I own with my sisters – we have been overwhelmed by the love and support people have shown us during this time. People, at their core, are so kind and really want to see their fellow humans succeed. It is truly beautiful.

I understand that this sounds like total Utopia, and I appreciate that this will not be everyone's perception of lockdown. Which brings me nicely to the main lesson I have learnt during my reflections: the lesson that we all get to choose to live in whatever thought-based reality we create for ourselves, due to us being in control of the energy we give to our thoughts.

The average human being has 80,000 thoughts every day. I often think that this can't be true – on the days where I am completely in my head and am think, think, thinking, I feel like I am more around the 80,000,000 mark. I have a LOT of thoughts.

I recently described the experience of when I am in my head to someone I was on a video call with. I described it as feeling like one of those conehead people from the movie called Coneheads (funnily enough).

Coneheads was a movie released in the 90s and the plot centred around a family of aliens who had heads shaped like cones (funnily enough, again).

On the days where I am in my head, I can physically feel my head expand to make room for all the additional thoughts that I am being bombarded with, and with this expansion it makes me feel like I would imagine a conehead person feels. The person who I was on the call with gave me a very strange look and hasn't contacted me again. Mmmmm, I wonder why?

Back to thought-based realities. Everything is created from thought. The thoughts we take on as real manifest as reality into our lives.

That said, if we have 80,000 thoughts every day, how can we possibly manifest 80,000 different situations and things every single day?

We can't. It is impossible.

Which leads to the assumption that a lot of the thoughts we have each and every day go unnoticed or disregarded – they do not create or manifest into a reality.

So, when and how do thoughts become things? How is our current reality shaped by certain thoughts, and if we are unhappy with our current reality, what control do we have over our thoughts?

A lot of questions, I know!

The good news is that it is all down to us and the choices we make in terms of which thoughts we choose to take on as being true.

We are solely responsible for the energy we give to our thoughts. We are in control of which thoughts we take on board and which thoughts we disregard. Most of this happens at a subconscious level, and a lot of thoughts have become hardwired as neural pathways in our minds.

Ultimately, we give energy to our thoughts by attaching emotion to the thought and having a physical response in our bodies to the thought as a result of previous experiences and past conditioning.

It works something like this:

1 - An experience or a situation occurs.

2 - Our brains generate a number of different thoughts as a way of processing the situation.

3 - We then very quickly feel the most dominant thought – an automatic, visceral response to this thought. We feel this as the emotion which is the most valid for us in that moment. Now, this can be a nice, warm, fuzzy feeling, which is lovely. It can also be an off feeling, as if something is just not quite right. At the other end of the spectrum, we can experience a feeling which is so raw and sore it feels as if someone has pushed their hand into your chest and tried to rip out your heart.

4 - Next, we conduct an internal verification test on whether the thought and feelings are valid or invalid, and we do this by basing it on our past experiences. If this internal test proves the thought to be invalid or not true, we generally move on to choose a new thought and test this thought out. You basically repeat this process until you find enough evidence to prove your thought to be valid.

5 - Once the thought has been validated, we proceed forward, feeling and behaving in a perfectly logical way based on the thought that we have validated in our head.

As I mentioned previously, this process is conducted on a subconscious level and happens in seconds. We can be forgiven if we believe that we have absolutely no control over it. When we believe that we have no control over it, it can be frustrating and debilitating, but it can also be freeing and liberating – depending on our mindset.

If we have what is often referred to as a positive mindset, working through the above process feels great because you subconsciously choose a thought that will leave you feeling warm, fuzzy, happy, in control and feeling that life is wonderful.

If, however, you are predisposed or conditioned to have a negative mindset, then you can often experience thoughts and feelings of despair, impending doom, fear, rejection, that life is hard and that if you didn't have bad luck, then you would have no luck at all! You might also believe that you have absolutely no control over your thoughts at all.

When I detailed the reality which I was experiencing earlier in the chapter – the reality where I felt like I had gone back in time – I realised that I was subconsciously choosing to attach to thoughts which were happy, contented, and peaceful.

I chose to breathe life into thoughts like, 'This experience is bringing families closer together,' 'Our beautiful planet is getting a chance to heal, as the pollution from planes is reducing,' and 'Local businesses will be able to survive the impact of this pandemic.'

Choosing these thoughts allowed me to experience the warm, fuzzy, lovely feelings which made me feel happy and at one with the world.

It could have quite easily gone the other way, and I could have subconsciously chosen different thoughts which would have changed my reality, my perception of the world. I could have thought, 'Bloody hell, it's rubbish that I am not going to get a summer holiday this year,' and 'Those kids of mine are doing my head in with their constant questions,' and even 'So what if the butchers and fruit shop is open? I want a new outfit from River Island and online isn't any good – I need to try things on.' These thoughts would have triggered feelings of discontent, disharmony and that the world was working against me. I would not be feeling like I was living my best life.

Here is the beautiful thing about thought-based realities that I have had the pleasure of understanding during lockdown: despite it all happening at a subconscious level, we are able to bring our thinking into the conscious level and make any necessary tweaks as required. We can change our mindset through creating a practice where we notice our thoughts for what they are. Without judgement, without attachment, with interested observation.

We can also choose which thoughts we want to attach emotions to, regardless of what our past experiences were. The past does not shape our future. This helps us to develop a practice where we can shift our mindset from being negative to positive – most of the time – and when we slip back to the negative mindset (which we inevitably will, sometimes), we can catch it quickly and take the necessary action required.

Finally, we can change our perception of what is going on in our lives and view it with gratitude, contentment, and love.

We do this by building a constant daily practice of awareness of our thoughts. When we notice a thought, we can introduce a pause before immediately accepting the thought to be true and ask ourselves the question, 'Will this thought serve me?' and 'Is this thought entirely valid at this point in time or am I making an assumption based on past experience?'

We can also ask 'What emotion will this thought make me feel?' and finally, 'Is there another thought I can have which will serve me better and make me feel happier?'

By asking ourselves these questions, we begin to challenge the thoughts which we are having, and we can choose to change them. The simple act of bringing awareness to our thoughts from a non-judgemental place depletes their power and provides a space in between thought and feeling.

Questions for Journaling and Reflection

- What have I noticed about my thoughts today?

- Are these thoughts valid?

- Are these thoughts serving me?

- What would be the positive opposite of the thoughts which are not serving me?

New Belief Statements for Thought-based Realities

- Every day in every way, I am getting better and better.

- I have everything I need to achieve my goals.

- My life is abundant on all levels.

- The Universe is a friendly place, providing everything I need.

- Everything is working out to the divine master plan.

Lesson 11:
Manifestation My Way

....

Ask, and it shall be given unto you;
Seek, and you shall find.
Knock, and it shall be opened unto you.
Hallelu, Hallelujah!

Journal Entry

Dear God,

- *I am a world-class coach, inspirational teacher and best-selling author, impacting and improving the lives of millions of people.*

- *I love me, and I am more than enough.*

- *I am healthy, happy and loving life.*

- *I am madly, deeply and passionately in love with my husband, Craig.*

- *I have a loving, connected relationship with my kids.*

- *I am deeply connected to my tribe. The people who get me as I get them.*

- *I have a massively successful online and in-person fitness and wellbeing company with my sister Joanna, where we get to powerfully serve our fitness family.*

- *I have a massively successful superfood company, which helps millions of people each year become healthier and happier.*

- *I am having fabulous fun, raising a fortune helping the world.*

This or something better. Thank you.

All my love always,
MC xxx

I have dabbled with the whole process of manifesting my deepest desires for about twenty years now, and I will admit that until last year I experienced feelings of deep resistance towards the process of it. Whenever I was asked to choose from the 'Universal Catalogue' or tasked with writing a list of what I would love to manifest in my life – I struggled. When I was encouraged to create a Vision Board or take part in some group manifestation programme – it never felt right to me.

My first struggle always appeared when I was asked to think about the things that I wanted. What kind of car do I want? What kind of house do I want to live in? How much money do I want to earn? What clothes do I want to wear, and where do I want to go on holiday?

In the past, I tried to overcome this resistance by writing down what I thought I was expected to write down, influenced somewhat by what society believes to be the right things to manifest – the 4x4, the five-bedroom house, the £50,000 savings in the bank, my mortgage paid off, etc.

I knew, though, on a deep, subconscious level that these things were, in actual fact, not what my heart desired – yet I still went along with the game.

During lockdown, I found a list of desires which I wrote down at the very first group personal development event I attended, over twenty years ago.

On the first day, we were asked to spend a bit of time writing a list of everything that we desired – our universal wish list. In the course materials, there was a section to complete this exercise, and there was space for fifty things that you would like to manifest into your life. I looked at the exercise – blankly – struggling to even find one thing to put down. What did I want?

I then had a moment of inspiration – I was single at the time and I knew deep in my heart that I wanted to find my soulmate and have a loving, respectful, fun partnership with my best friend for the rest of my life. I put that down on the list – then returned again to the struggle of what else could I put down on the list.

In amongst the background music, which was designed to stimulate and unleash our manifestation creation powers, the person hosting the event was giving suggestions. He was asking us to consider what kind of house we wanted to live in, places we wanted to visit, how much money we would like to earn, cars that we would like to drive, clothes we wished to buy.

In the absence of having nothing else to write I latched onto these suggestions and put down things like a Golf GTI convertible (they were cool at the time), a boat for my dad, my own mansion, a size ten body, run a marathon, a £40,000 a year salary, a trip around the world, etc.

The purpose of this exercise was to start the ball rolling towards creating an amazing life for yourself. It was an exercise in visualisation, asking you to determine what you needed in order to make you happy, fulfilled and living your best life. Deep within my heart, I knew at the time that getting the 'things' would not bring me lasting happiness, inner peace and a sense of complete and utter fulfilment.

Yet, at the time, I did not know what else to do. There was a guy up on the stage telling me that I had to think of fifty 'things' that I wanted and that if I got those 'things' then I would be happy, and I would be living my best life.

I really struggled, and having found the list recently, most of the things which I put on that list have never materialised into my real world … with the exception of the size ten body (when I starve myself for a month), meeting my soul mate (first thing on the list) … and my Dad's boat, which I am pretty sure was down to his own manifestation powers.

This pattern of writing a wish list to the Universe has been something that I have done at least once a year with very little success since then. In 2019, I attended the Unleash the Power Within event, which is run by the incredible powerhouse that is Tony Robbins. He conducted the same exercise as the one I described above, asking the audience to write down what we wanted. He also popped on the nice music and started making suggestions of things that we could write down. The cars, the houses, the holidays, finances … and again I experienced the struggle, as my old friend resistance popped up to say hello.

My inner voice was saying, 'I don't know what "things" I want to manifest; I have no idea what my dream car or dream house would be.' And for the first time ever in all the many times of doing this exercise, I listened to this inner voice, this inner wisdom and guidance. I listened to it with love and respect, and I asked it, 'Ok, what do you want to manifest, what will allow you to feel like you are living your best life?' I went silent and allowed whatever to come up, understanding that this would be my truth.

This is what I wrote:

> *'An extraordinary life for me, my life at the next level would be
> me living in abundance. An abundance of health, happiness,
> love, connection and finances. I would feel in flow, connected to
> God. I would feel light of spirit. I would smile, laugh, be
> playful. I would love myself exactly as I am, and I would be
> working on my true goals – the things that truly matter to me.'*

It came to me in that instant – this is exactly what I want to
manifest. This is what will make my heart sing and allow me to
feel like I am operating and contributing at the very highest
level. What also came through to me very strongly was a deep
belief that this was happening – that what I truly wanted to
manifest would be brought into reality. I would be feeling
abundant in health, happiness, love, connection and finances,
working in a state of flow, connected to God, working towards
my true goals – the things that matter to me and to the world.

I feel the need to point out here that I do also like the 'things'.
I love it when I see a new pair of trainers that I have ordered
being delivered, and the feeling of walking into a beautiful
hotel room in a lovely hotel at the start of a holiday is
incredible.

I am materialistic to a point.

What I have noticed, however, is that the manifestation of the
'things' only brings me temporary joy – it is a nice feeling
when it arrives, but the feeling doesn't hang around for very
long.

Like with any valuable lesson in life, we often have to be
taught it (or reminded of it) a few times before the lesson sticks.

During lockdown, I have found myself slipping back to how I

was encouraged to manifest in the past – signing up for group programmes and reading books which encourage me to focus on the achievement of the 'things', as opposed to what will make my heart sing and create lasting feelings of true abundance in my life.

On a recent programme, I wrote down that I wanted to be mortgage-free by the end of October 2020. When I think on this, I do not actually care whether I am mortgage-free. Being mortgage-free will not make my heart sing with joy, and I also didn't believe that it would happen by October 2020. (FYI – it hasn't!)

The time in lockdown has taught me this valuable lesson about the magic of manifestation again. It is my hope that by having this completely and utterly insightful revelation once again, I will remember it for the rest of my life. This will allow me to tap into the correct way to manifest my heart's deepest desires, trusting that when the right conditions for success are in place, then it will work very quickly. By remembering this lesson, I will be able to share it with all who will listen, enabling them to live a life of abundance – abundance in everything that makes them feel that they are living life at the highest level.

The lesson came in the shape of the manifestation of a scholarship intensive with Michael Neill (author of Supercoach and The Inside Out Revolution). I have been following the teachings of Michael for a while and feel a massive connection – he is a kindred spirit. I love how he brings spirituality into his coaching and how he has a deep belief that we are all being guided and that all we have to do is witness the times when we are moving away from a feeling of complete and utter wellbeing. He teaches that we do not have to try to fix it, we do not have to blame anyone or anything, and we certainly do not have to beat ourselves up for it.

He shares the same belief as I do that we were all born perfect, with feelings of true happiness, peace and joy, and that we can all return to this God-like state whenever we wish through simply recognising that a thought is just a thought and we feel bad or good depending on the energy we give to these thoughts.

If we attach energy or emotion to thoughts which do not serve us, then we will move away from our birth-right feelings of being loved and being good enough, the way we deserve to feel every single day.

One night during lockdown, I treated myself to an Epsom salt bath as an act of self-care and love towards myself, whilst I finished Michael Neill's book The Inside Out Revolution. At the end of the book was a list of recommended resources for the reader to tap into to deepen their learning. I tend to skim past this part of any book.

On this occasion, however, I was drawn to Michael's Supercoach website, so I picked up my phone and typed the website address into my browser. The first thing that came up on the website was an online intensive that Michael was running later that week called 'The Genius Catalyst Intensive'.

I looked at it with fascination and watched the video reviews on previous intensives, and I got this feeling of excitement rising up in me. My inner voice said, 'This would be awesome, you would get so much from this.' I then saw the cost, and the rational part of me said, 'Maybe another time, it probably isn't a good idea to spend $500 on a course at the moment, is it?' My heart sank.

Another section of the website then caught my eye. It announced that Michael was offering fifty scholarship places – FREE places – for the event. It advised that he was accepting applications from individuals who were doing their bit to help others during the Covid-19 global pandemic.

My inner voice piped up again, saying, 'This is you, you should apply, you are helping people through the coaching that you are doing for the local council, and you are helping people through the delivery of your free fitness and yoga sessions that you and Joanna are teaching online.'

So, before I allowed the inner critic to come in and do her unhappy dance and telling me that I was a fraud and that I wasn't really helping anyone, I clicked onto the link to apply – I got out of my head and tapped into my heart space. I wrote about what I was doing in my small corner of the world, and how I believed that I would be able to share my learnings from the intensive with anyone who was willing to listen. I even spoke about my calling in Rome to write this book.

I hit send and said a prayer to God to make it be so.

Now, here is the thing about manifesting what you truly desire. It is absolutely crucial to FEEL how amazing it will be when the thing you are manifesting comes into your reality. Even more so, it is important to feel as if you already have the thing and experience what will be going on in your body and mind when it happens. When I thought about receiving an email advising me that I had won a scholarship onto the intensive, I was buzzing with feelings of happiness, joy, gratitude, excitement and accomplishment. I was vibrating on a really high energy.

Looking back to all those times when I was writing all those lists of 'things', I did not FEEL that I was vibrating on this super high energy. I was not buzzing with excitement, joy, gratitude and accomplishment.

I know now that I didn't really want the 'things' – I was trying to convince myself that I did.

The second thing which I noticed is that I BELIEVED in my heart and soul that it was actually possible for me to be successful in gaining this scholarship. Furthermore, I BELIEVED it was probable and that I would be accepted. I also BELIEVED (at that moment in time) that I was indeed worth it. I felt like I deserved to get the scholarship.

The final thing that I became consciously aware of was that I RELEASED it. I handed it over to God, and if He decided that this was the right thing for me, then it would happen – the stars would align, and I would receive word that I was being granted a scholarship. I RELEASED with trust in God.

I would like to say that after I released my desire with trust in God that I actually did just that – the reality was that I did not. I am human, after all. Over the next few days, I continually thought about it, I checked my emails way more than I normally do, and the traffic to Michael Neill's website probably increased about 100% during that time.

When I noticed myself doing this, I repeated the mantra, 'If it is meant to be, it will be,' and I released my desire once again into the hands of God. The repeating and the releasing exercise happened a LOT during the period from when I submitted the application to when I heard.

Now, this would be a pretty pointless story and pretty cruel to boot if I was to write telling you that I did not get accepted. I am delighted to say that this story is neither pointless, nor is it cruel. The stars were aligned, and my heart's desire was realised. I received an email advising me that my application had been considered and that they would love to offer me a scholarship on the programme.

I am a Magic Manifestor!

On reflection of the actions I subconsciously took in the manifestation of this scholarship, I took the time to look back on my life and was reminded of numerous instances where I adopted the exact same process to manifest what I truly wanted.

Sometimes the manifestation happened really quickly, other times it took a little bit longer. To manifest my caravan in my favourite place in the world, it took a couple of weeks, whereas to manifest my soulmate Craig, it took a few years. The lesson I take from this is that your heart and soul need to really want the thing that you are asking for, and God has to decide when the time is right for you to receive it. And that is perfectly ok with me.

Feel into your heart's desire, believe that it is happening and you are worthy, then release with trust and faith to God.

Questions for Journaling and Reflection

- What do I truly desire?

- Do I believe that it is possible and that I am worthy of it? In what way?

- How can I release any blocks which are in the way of me receiving my heart's desire?

- In what ways can I release my heart's desire to God with faith and trust?

New Belief Statements For Manifesting

- My life is abundant on all levels.

- I can create the life I truly want to live.

- It is safe, fun and easy to manifest my hearts desires.

- I experience harmony in mind, body, and spirit.

- Every day in every way, my life is amazing.

Lesson 12:
Stop, Notice, and Change

....

Do not be afraid, for I have redeemed you.
I have called you by your name; you are mine.
When you walk through the waters, I'll be with you,
You will never sink beneath the waves.

<u>Journal Entry</u>

Dear God,

Today, I am freaking WINNING. I am a complete and utter rockstar at this home-schooling, homeworking, home-running malarkey. It is a complete and utter piece of piss – pardon my French (because I now know French on account of the kick-ass French lesson I taught this morning).

Yesterday – not so much!! I got all into my head before my online class and let the fear come in, which turned me into a total anxious, crabbit psycho bitch and whilst practising yoga relaxed me a lot – did I mention YOGA was KING? – I was still a bit on edge afterwards. So, I did what I mostly always do in these situations. I had my dinner, went mute and then fell into bed, exhausted mentally and physically.

Today, however, I am a legend!! And I have got this!

'coronacoaster'
noun
the ups and downs of a person's mood, or life generally,
during the coronavirus pandemic

On awakening that particular morning of that journal entry, I felt fearful, on account of all the psycho-bitchness I had displayed the previous evening, and I started to ruminate on all the things that were going wrong. I then turned to my old friend catastrophisation and went down various different rabbit holes of old negative beliefs and stories I had created over the years.

You know, the really juicy stories like:

'My marriage isn't as solid as I thought, he doesn't understand me, maybe we would be better splitting up,'

and

'My friends don't even like me. I haven't heard from such and such for weeks. She doesn't care,'

to

'What am I even thinking about doing this online group. No-one wants to watch me doing a class. I am rubbish at it. Everyone loves my sister, and no one likes me.'

I remember that morning very well. That was the morning where I was able to take some control back of my emotions.

Being in lockdown took most of us on an emotional rollercoaster ride, where one day we were feeling on top of the world, then the next we were in the depths of despair – experiencing extreme emotional highs and nasty lows.

That was the morning I remembered to STOP, NOTICE, and CHANGE.

The STOP, NOTICE, and CHANGE Method starts with an awareness of feeling off-kilter, that feeling of something being not just quite right.

It may be a feeling of anxiousness or even a sense of having a dark cloud hanging over your head. In that moment of awareness, we have to say 'STOP' out loud. This shakes up those neural pathways in our minds, which are set to run on default.

The next step is to physically STOP everything we are doing and ask ourselves the following questions. It is very beneficial to journal on these to get true insights:

1 - What emotion am I feeling?

By naming the emotion, you are able to take the power away from it to a large extent.

2 - What thoughts am I having that I am breathing life into?

We generally always feel before we notice the thoughts we are having, and often we do not join the dots between the two. Thoughts and emotions are so interlinked, and often our understanding is that we have no control over our thoughts – and this to a certain extent is true. Remember, we have about 80,000 thoughts every day – we cannot be expected to control every one of them. It is the feelings and emotions which we attach to the thoughts that cause us to experience a wide range of both positive and negative feelings and emotions.

For example, when I am experiencing happiness, I feel happiness by feeling that I am open, light and carefree in body and mind – as if the world is looking out for me. My thoughts will generally be hopeful and optimistic, and I will see the good in others and in myself.

If, however, I am experiencing anger, well, that is a different set of feelings. I might physically feel hot or have tightness across my chest, and my thoughts will be that everything and everyone is against me, that no one understands me, and that external factors are to blame.

By noticing the thoughts which are attached to the feelings and emotions – as quickly as we can, especially when the feelings are of the non-serving variety (early intervention is always best) – we can proceed on to the next step.

3 - Are these thoughts 100% valid?

A great way to figure this out is by doing a list of reasons for and reasons against, in as objective a way as you can. If I feel that I can't be objective in doing this step, then I always enlist the help of someone I trust.

Whenever I have done this validation exercise, I generally realise that my thoughts are not 100% valid. Often times, especially when I am a victim of monthly hopping hormones, I establish that they aren't even 10% valid – ooops!!

On the occasions where I have found that the thoughts are 100% valid, I have realised that this is still a very useful exercise to carry out, as I now have a starting point for change. If I am feeling anger, and I establish that I am 100% valid in having that feeling in that moment, I now have a clear picture of how I do not want to think or feel. No-one ever really wants to feel anger or other such low vibration emotions.

From this place, I can start to take action.

If I choose not to take action – then that is on me. If I were in a place where I was continuously feeling the lower vibrational feelings and doing nothing about it, then I need to realise that there is no Fairy Godmother out there who is going to wave her magic wand and grant me three wishes. I have to step up and make changes on a daily basis to raise my emotional vibration.

4 - What new thought can I have?

From the validation list, I then get to decide to change the thought if the thought I am having is not serving me, and I know that I would prefer to experience more positive feelings.

I ask myself – 'What new thought could I have instead of the thought I am currently having?'

By consciously changing the thought, I consciously change my state (in some instances, changing my physiology helps too) and my feelings and emotions lift to a higher vibrational state. It is actually that simple; it can be difficult at times, however. With practice and repetition, it does become a lot easier.

This whole process does not take long at all – so, please do not be put off by the lengthy instructions. Changing our physiology speeds the process up even further, on the basis that a body in movement vibrates at a higher frequency and emotional state than a sedentary body.

Back to my journal entry:

After utilising the STOP, NOTICE, and CHANGE method, I am delighted to report that I was able to change my state on awakening from feeling despair, and feeling rejected and unloved to feeling hopeful, in control and connected. Go me.

I got up, quickly got dressed, popped the leash on Dusty Dog, and Craig and I took him out for a walk.

Getting outside, being in the moment, watching Dusty's happy wee face as he chased after seagulls (and the occasional car wheel) without a care in the world, with his happy doggy smile on his lips really lifted my vibration even further. I always thought that the saying, 'It's a dog's life' was a negative thing – turns out, it's the bloody opposite. Dogs have the right idea – eat, sleep, chase seagulls – sorted!

By the time I was home, had a coffee and some brekkie, I was ME again, positively buzzing. I owned the day.

Thank you.

All my love always,
MC xxx

It starts and ends with us. We are responsible for which thoughts we allow to affect our emotional state, and we are responsible for changing the thought when necessary.

Questions for Journaling and Reflection

- What emotion am I feeling at this moment in time?

- What thoughts am I breathing life into that are driving this emotion?

- Are these thoughts 100% valid?

- What would be the positive opposite of this thought, and how valid is this?

New Belief Statements for Stop, Notice, and Change

- I am in control of my thoughts.

- I am worthy of thinking good thoughts and feeling good emotions.

- I can change my state whenever I need to.

- I experience harmony in mind, body, and spirit.

- I forgive and release the conditioning from past experiences.

Lesson 13:
We Never Fail

....

Colours of day dawn into the mind,
The sun has come up, the night is behind.
Go down in the city, into the street,
And let's give the message to the people we meet.

<u>Journal Entry</u>

Dear God,

The lessons I have learnt today:

- *Being presented with an opportunity to fail is a gift from you.*

- *That it is ok to fail, but it is not ok to fail to learn the lesson.*

- *By failing, I will grow as an individual and will be able to show up and contribute to the world more powerfully.*

- *Sometimes there is a better plan for me than the one I was working towards, and I must be open to this.*

- *Family yoga is actually really good fun.*

My intentions going forward from these lessons:

- *When I 'fail', I will slow down. I won't worry. I will become quiet, and I will tap into my inner wisdom, which will tell me the solution and what to do.*

- *Recruit Maria as my yoga side-kick.*

Thank you for this lesson.

All my love always,
MC xxx

During Lockdown I failed………..a lot!!

Specific failures included not being able to live stream a yoga class when I was scheduled to do one. The technology just did not want to play ball, and despite trying for half an hour to get it working, it wouldn't let me. This meant that my Thursday yogis did not get their yoga fix.

I also failed one of my customers and friends from high school. He is a massive fan of the superfood powder blends which I have created and sings their praises for keeping people healthy and strong. I found out during lockdown that he was really ill for a couple of weeks and had all the symptoms of Covid-19. The meaning I gave to this was that my superfood powder blends did not keep his immune system strong enough to prevent him from getting the virus or even keeping his symptoms relatively mild.

I failed my kids by not keeping my shit together. More times than I care to remember or document.

BC (Before Coronavirus), my default reaction to these 'failures' would generally involve a whole lot of beating myself up, thinking 'What's the point?', self-flagellation, taking my disappointment in myself out on those close to me by being irritable and withdrawn, and generally wallowing in the lower vibrational state of blame, shame, and guilt.

Lockdown granted me the opportunity to turn this whole feeling of being a failure whenever something goes wrong on its head.

Thank you, lockdown.

When the technology stopped being my friend, something in me said, 'It doesn't matter. Don't worry, there is a reason for this,' and because of my new-found ability to slow down, to become quiet and to listen to the inner voice that wants to guide me – I did exactly that. I slowed down instead of frantically pressing every single button on the keyboard to try to 'fix' it.

I also didn't worry – because in the big scale of things it wasn't really the end of the world. I became silent – trusting that the voice would guide me as to the best course of action. And, I listened – the voice gave me a solution.

I popped a message onto the group page, apologising. I made a joke about how it seemed like my technology was also on lockdown that evening, and I advised them all that I would deliver a yoga class the following day.

The response I got from the community was amazing. They were so understanding and accepting of the situation, and they all loved the fact that there was going to be a live class the following day.

I then had a brainwave. An idea popped into my head that I should make the class suitable for families. My daughter Maria agreed (after a certain degree of persuasion) to come on live with me and together we would deliver the class, making it as fun as possible.

The group LOVED the idea, and I ended up having double the number of people join the class. An added bonus was that Maria and I had such a giggle doing the live class together – it was so much fun.

The icing on the cake was that the feedback from both parents and their kids was incredible – it blew me away. Everyone who took part said that they loved it, and that it was exactly what they needed. One of my beautiful yogi friends said that she had been having such a low day that day, and the class completely lifted her spirits.

The situation reminded me of the saying, 'Sometimes on the way to a dream, you get lost and find a better one.'

Not being able to deliver the originally planned class did not mean that I was a failure. I completely believe in my heart now that it was meant to happen. If the technology had worked for me and I had been able to deliver the original class, it would have given my Thursday yogis their yoga fix.

An opportunity would have been lost, however, for me to deliver a family class which allowed so many people to de-stress, connect and have fun on a dreary, drizzly Friday afternoon.

It wasn't a failure – it was a WIN.

In terms of my good friend and how ill he was, I quickly realised that I could not take responsibility or blame for his illness; this would not serve him in any shape or form. Nor would it serve me. This was not a failure on my part. I quickly understood that I could not take on the belief that my blends of superfood powders are ineffective in keeping the immune system strong. I trust and believe that they are.

There are so many other variables which could have contributed to his immune system being low – he had started ultra-running a few months previously, he was travelling all over the world prior to lockdown, and he had a job where he was in contact with lots and lots of people.

I am so relieved and thankful that he recovered, and on speaking to him, he is now taking a holistic view to his wellness – looking at the various factors of diet, fitness, sleep, and stress.

Another win!

The thing about perceived failure is that we all too often attribute negative connotations to it – we believe that it is something that we do not want to happen to us. I now am of the opinion that failure, in fact, should be seen as a positive thing. It should be embraced, sought out and anticipated with positive expectation. Welcomed in with open arms when it arrives.

Failure gives us the opportunity to learn and grow with the belief that nothing worthwhile was ever learnt on a good day. When I look back over my life, it was the times when everything went completely and utterly tits-up that I was granted the opportunity to up-level and grow. It was my darkest days where I was able to find an inner strength, an inner knowledge and the courage to pick myself up, dust myself down, and show up to the world like the badass freaking rockstar that I am at my core.

As a coach, I encourage clients to go out and 'fail'. I do this because going out and doing something, even if it goes belly-up, is far better than staying stuck doing nothing. A life filled with regret and 'if only' is far less fulfilling than a life filled with lessons as a result of us getting it wrong. We become far more resilient and have much more of a blast as a result of living this way.

And as we grow as individuals on account of all these lessons, we become more able to show up and contribute more fully to this world.

During lockdown, I have been able to look differently at so many situations when things did not go as I had originally intended. I now see that being presented with an opportunity to fail is a gift from God, and that it is ok to fail. It is not ok, however, to fail to learn the lesson. I also appreciate that by failing, I will grow as an individual and will be able to show up and contribute to the world much more powerfully.

As a mother, the times I have failed with my children during lockdown have helped me to learn, grow and become better. After lockdown, the kids resumed school. When they returned home after their first day back, I asked them how they had enjoyed it. Their unanimous reply was that it was so much better than being home-schooled by me. This was my biggest win of all. I had failed so miserably at being a teacher, my kids now loved and were grateful for school so much more. Result!

Finally, I also accept that sometimes God has a better plan for me than the one I am working towards; it is my intention to be always open to this.

Questions for Journaling and Reflection

- How do I view failure?

- What lessons have I learnt as a result of failing in my life?

- In which areas am I holding myself back as a result of the fear of failure?

- How can I view my failures differently?

New Belief Statements for When We Fail

- It's ok for me to make mistakes.

- I trust that everything is unfolding exactly as it should.

- I am learning my lessons with love and compassion.

- Every day in every way, I am getting better and better.

- My mistakes are an opportunity for me to learn and grow.

Lesson 14:
The Tricks of The Trade

....

O Lord, my God, when I in awesome wonder
Consider all the worlds Thy Hands have made,
I see the stars, I hear the rolling thunder,
Thy power throughout the universe displayed.

Journal Entry

Cue tumbleweed!!! Ooops!!

For some strange (slightly crazy, if you ask me) reason, a couple of months into lockdown, I stopped a lot of my daily practices – the practices and routines which I have learned, created and honed over the last twenty years, which keep me buzzing mentally and physically.

For what reason I stopped, I do not know, nor am I wasting my precious time questioning this. Do we ever know why we do something that does not serve us? All I know is that by not committing the time to my daily routines and practices, I noticed that I was starting to slip into fearful feelings and thoughts and buying into the whole negative energy that is a dominant force in the world at the moment.

'Your Pal Boris' announced on Sunday 10 May 2020 that he

was relaxing the lockdown measures – he advised that if we could not work from home, then we should think about returning to our normal place of work. We could go out for unlimited amounts of exercise, and we could meet with one other person who did not live in our house – providing that we adhered to social distancing measures. He set out a phased plan for returning to a new normal in the UK and gave timescales for when we should expect to jump back onto our respective hamster wheels and return to the hustle and bustle of frantic Western world living (my words, not his).

He gave timelines for children returning to school as well as when shops, pubs, restaurants and leisure facilities could open their doors to the great British public again.

The end is nigh …

Nicola Sturgeon – the First Minister for Scotland – came onto our TV screens promptly after Boris and said, 'Do not listen to that bloody idiot: stay home, stay safe, and protect our NHS. You can, however, go outside to exercise on your own or with members of your family more than once a day. Woe betide anyone who listens to Boris, and not to me' (again my words, not hers – I am slightly scared of Nicola).

The end is not nigh …

This news affected me in two ways. On the one hand, I was really happy to keep my hamster wheel gathering dust in the place that I had abandoned it gleefully. I was so happy in my bubble of deep connection with my family tribe, doing whatever, whenever and for however long I chose to. The thought of having to start rushing around like a hamster on speed again, from one gig to the next, whilst juggling a million different plates did not fill me with excitement.

On the other hand, on account of my lack of commitment to my daily practices, I became fearful of the future of our business and began heading down the rabbit hole of catastrophic thinking, picking up shards of potential evidence to validate the demise of the dream empire along the way.

My List of Catastrophic Thoughts

- Clients will never come back to the classes because they have been away too long.

- Numbers are down on the online live classes on the online group.

- We aren't getting the same amount of engagement on the group.

- There haven't been any sales today of my superfood blends.

- The way Nicola is talking, we won't be allowed to open the gym ever again.

- Who will want to pay for coaching at a time like this? Everyone is watching their finances.

- The way the world is going, Craig's company will fold. He will lose his job, and we will have to live in a cardboard box out in the street.

- My kids are going to end up behind on their education with all the school they have missed.

- What is wrong with me, I can't stop eating chocolate and crisps?

The glass-half-empty list could go on and on – I will save you from it!

My inner guide then whispered, 'When was the last time you wrote in your journal?'

I stopped, I reflected and realised that it was over a week ago. The voice asked, louder this time, 'What about setting your daily intention?' – again, over a week ago. Louder still, 'And what about fuelling your body for success? How is that going?' I was midway through my third chocolate bar that day, and I had eaten a Scotch pie for my lunch – you can make your own assumptions on the answer to that question.

I realised that I had abandoned/stopped/forgotten my daily practices. The non-negotiables that I committed to doing most days to keep my mind and body primed – to allow me to be my best self, feel my best, and show up every day doing my best.

I could have spent time exploring, evaluating, questioning and berating myself for stopping these practices. For allowing myself to turn to the dark side – but what benefit would there have been in that? How would that have helped me and allowed me to feel better? It would not have facilitated a return to my desired state of innate wellbeing, the place where the warm, fuzzy, optimistic, happy feelings reside.

Instead, I praised myself for noticing that the internal emotional thermostat that we all have had changed to a temperature which I was not comfortable with. In bringing awareness to this, I could also bring acceptance to it and ask myself a question: do I want my internal emotional thermostat to return to my desired temperature?

The answer was an obvious YES – I craved a return to the warm, fuzzy, happy place.

Next question – what could I do to help this return?

Answer – I can accept what is, begin to remove what is not serving me (goodbye my chocolatey love), and reintroduce what does.

In that moment, after I finished the multipack (obviously), I picked up my journal, and I wrote and wrote and wrote. On completion, my vibration felt a lot lighter. The wellbeing thermostat had returned to the desired temperature.

I love journaling. It really helps me to get everything out of my body and mind. I write about the emotions I am experiencing, the thoughts I am having, the worries and thoughts my mind is conjuring up, and the fears that I have. I get it all out by scribbling away – sometimes for five minutes, sometimes for an hour. It really helps dispel the stressful feelings and thoughts I am having – EVERY SINGLE TIME!

Interestingly, a study was carried out on the effectiveness of expressive writing (another name for journaling) for individuals who had experienced trauma in their lives, and I firmly believe that the period of time where we were in lockdown will be classed as a traumatic event. The group who took part in the study completed some form of expressive writing for just fifteen minutes every day. After just a week, the majority of them experienced feelings of increased wellbeing, felt less stressed, and could look to the future with a degree of hope.

Another interesting by-product of the study was that the individual's immune systems became stronger.

There are a number of ways that you can journal, from simply free-writing to using some prompts such as Wisdom Access Questions, which really help to tap into your inner wisdom – the God within.

Wisdom Access Questions were first introduced to me when I trained to become a life coach in 2015. They formed an integral part of my coaching toolkit, which allowed me to enable the client to reach greater insights, gain clarity over a situation and increase self-awareness. A wisdom access question generally starts with the word 'What' and examples are, 'What's stopping you?' 'What would make the biggest difference here?' 'What do you hope to accomplish by taking this action?' and, 'What's the first step?' A full list of Wisdom Access Questions can be found on the internet.

My preferred way to journal, as you will have gathered by now, is by writing a letter to God. I obviously start the letter with 'Dear God', because how else would you start a letter to God? I practice gratitude by thanking Him for all the good that happened that day. I follow this by detailing what I have done well – this is especially important on the days that I just don't feel like I am winning. By taking the time to reflect and note it down, I soon realise that I have achieved far more than I give myself credit for. I finish by sending love, light, and forgiveness to the shadow side of me, recognising and accepting these parts of me that lower my vibration, the parts of me that I have hidden and suppressed for so long.

This whole exercise takes approximately ten minutes, and yet it feels like you have had five hours worth of therapy. It is so powerful and healing, especially so when I do it before bed. It allows me to brain-dump all the thoughts, feelings, and emotions that I would generally ruminate over whilst trying to get to sleep.

Another tool which I always love to use is writing and saying affirmation statements. I AM statements are so powerful. What comes after the I AM really shapes how I see myself and how I present myself to the world. For more years than I care to remember, I have played the I AM FAT statement over and over in my head. I spoke about it at length in the Body Love lesson. Before I learned how powerful I AM statements are in shaping my destiny, I AM FAT was a mantra that I repeated to myself every time I looked in the mirror and whenever I had the opportunity to say it out loud.

Whenever someone would compliment me on an outfit, rather than thanking them for going out of their way to say something nice to me, I would say, 'Really, do I not look fat in it?' and whenever I tried a new outfit on, I would say to the nearest person (usually poor Craig), 'What do you think of this? Does it make me look fat?' This happened A LOT, so often, in fact, that my subconscious mind bought into it and created a hard-wired belief. The belief that I was, in fact, fat. I didn't even have to consciously think it anymore – it became part of what I did and how I thought. After a long time, I started to realise that this particular affirmation did not serve and that I wanted to release it (with love and light, of course), and in its place create a belief that enabled me to feel and look great – whatever I was wearing or not wearing. The mantra I created was I LOOK AND FEEL FANTASTIC.

In the beginning, I did not buy into this affirmation one tiny bit; however, with continual repetition, verbally and in writing, with complete faith, belief and hope, I started to shift my perception of myself. I also asked for help from God because I knew deep in my heart that He did not want me to feel like that about myself. It is still a work in progress, but with every day I am moving closer and closer to that place. It is becoming my new hard-wired belief.

Another affirmation that is on daily repeat is I AM A CONFIDENT, CAPABLE COACH, INSPIRATIONAL TEACHER AND BEST-SELLING AUTHOR IMPACTING AND IMPROVING THE LIVES OF MILLIONS OF PEOPLE. I am saying and writing this with complete faith, belief and hope – trusting that if it is God's will, then it will be so.

A Gratitude Diary is a major player in my toolkit and has given me so much comfort during this period of time when it could have been so easy to focus on what was not going right in the world. Living in a state of gratitude for what we have been blessed with is the highest state on the emotional vibration scale and allows us to see the world as the wonderful, beautiful, incredible place that it is.

I normally practise gratitude in the evening just before I go to bed by listing ten things that I am grateful to God for that day. It can be something as small as being grateful for toothpaste, which allows my mouth to be all nice and fresh, to the deep love I feel for my husband and kids. I express gratitude for the things I currently have in life, as well as the things that are coming my way.

I always finish my gratitude list feeling so appreciative for the life I have been blessed with.

No feel-good toolkit would be complete without meditation. Sitting in silence, consciously breathing and meditating has been an absolute gift to me, and I am so happy and grateful that it found me. I am an all-round happier, more balanced person when I regularly take the time out to meditate. Granting myself permission to stop, to sit in silence, to meditate into a candle or even listen to a guided meditation is so powerful. It is vital for keeping my mental wellbeing in a good place. I try to meditate every night and most mornings – sometimes for five minutes, sometimes twenty – and firmly believe that it helps keep me calm, focussed, and liking myself a lot more. I show up much better as the real authentic me when I have had quiet time.

When I do not give myself the gift of meditation, I notice myself becoming slightly unravelled and just not ME. For a while, I believed it was the meditation that was 'fixing' me. I now understand that it wasn't. It was the physical act of giving myself space to consciously breathe, to notice my thoughts, without judgement, without attachment. To sit in the place between thought and feeling and allowing myself to decide whether I wanted to breathe energy into certain thoughts I was having, whether I wanted to take them on, to attach a feeling to them, and generate a specific behaviour. It is hard to do this when I am caught up in the business of life. I really need and benefit from a few minutes to do nothing, slow down and tap into my thoughts.

As previously mentioned, the period of time during lockdown was described as a 'coronacoaster' – the name given to the emotional rollercoaster of feelings we experienced. One day we were on top of the world, a bit bleugh the next, then feeling downright depressed the following. Each new day seemed to bring with it a lucky dip of emotions, and what we picked from the dip determined how we were feeling that day. During lockdown, all over social media, people were being the most honest they have ever been and admitted when they were feeling low and having a 'down day'. In a way, it was so refreshing to see after years of being bombarded by the shiny, filtered, 'look at how perfect my life is', fake-ness of it all.

Through leaning in and admitting how we are truly feeling, we can accept, embrace, and forgive, and are able to move through it a whole lot quicker. By becoming more honest with what is going on, by accepting the feeling for what it is, we are able to take away some of its power. We can begin to tap into our inner wisdom and be guided as to the best thing for us to do at any given moment in time. Additionally, by putting our authentic, true selves out there to the world, we give permission to others to do the same.

Fuelling my body is another key tool which I need to implement, allowing me to feel my best mentally and physically.

The period of time during lockdown was likened to being on holiday from work, without the heading off to sunnier climes, for obvious reasons. The Government's recommendation was for us to stay at home where possible, and work from home where we could. Where this was not possible, the people who do not work in jobs which are classed as essential were put on what is called furlough (yet another word that we never gave so much as a second thought to last year).

The Furlough Scheme was introduced by the government to prevent many people from being made redundant on account of their companies not being able to trade and operate in their usual way. Employees of these companies were asked to stay at home, and in return, the government paid them 80% of their usual salary. On speaking to employees who have been furloughed, a lot of them reported that it felt like they were getting free money and that they were on holiday. A few companies who had a good cash flow topped up the remaining 20% so that their employees did not suffer any financial detriment. The theory of it sounded too good to be true, and the rabbit hole of where the government was getting all the money to pay the furloughed employees was a hole that I avoided going down.

Lockdown, where you were either furloughed or working from home, could be likened to the time off that some of us have at Christmas (without the presents, the sequins and having to dance to 'Well I Wish it Could Be Christmas Every Day', pretending that we love the song). It was so easy to turn night into day and to stop following the usual daily structure that having a job to show up for gives us.

What generally always happens to me around the Christmas break time is that my commitment to fuelling my body with nutrient-dense food kind of gets forgotten and I end up feeling sluggish, bloated, not firing on all cylinders, and flat.

In my reflections, that day when I noticed these same feelings creeping in, I realised that my daily intention to fuel my body for optimum health and vitality was not being met with the required daily actions. And that whilst I love the taste of a Cadbury Twirl (or five) with a cup of coffee mid-afternoon, I recognised that it would not serve me well in the long term. I also noticed that if I do not take my superfood powders daily, get lots of fruit and veggies in, and drink at least a couple of litres of water a day, then I am not enabling myself to be my best or feel my best.

When I realised this, I noticed that I had stopped listening to what my body truly wanted and needed. I had turned the volume down on the inner nutritionist that we all have inside us — the inner wisdom which tells me what nutrients I need at any point in time. I had stopped eating intuitively.

Until about ten years ago, I had an unhealthy relationship with food. Something clicked in me, and I took back the power I had given away to the diet industry for most of my adult life. From around the age of fourteen, I had been on some diet or another (some crazier than others), and I definitely categorised foods as Good or Bad. I was also consumed with guilt every time I ate something that wasn't on the particular plan which I was following at that time.

With teaching so many classes every week and entering into the joyful peri-menopausal stage of my life, I really had to take stock of how I was fuelling my body — and by doing this stock take, I noticed that my relationship with food wasn't the greatest.

It required a complete overhaul of my thinking around food – and as the experience during lockdown taught me, it is still a work in progress. I make it my intention to see food as fuel. I adopt an 80/20 rule where I eat nutrient-dense foods most of the time and allow myself chocolate, crisps, and beer on occasion – because I love the taste of them!

I committed to tuning into my body and eating intuitively – trusting that my body knows what it wants and needs. I realised that I did not need some multi-billion-dollar money-making industry to tell me this.

Eating intuitively gives me the energy to power through my week and stops me feeling like I am depriving myself of anything. I also feel more in control and love ME a hell of a lot more!!

The final cog in the wheel of my mental and physical wellbeing success is fitness. I consider myself one of the lucky ones. I really enjoy exercising. I have for as long as I can remember. I love the feeling that I get during and after a run. I love how strong I feel during a weight session and how connected to my body and mind I am during a yoga class. Doing something physically active not only keeps me fit and healthy – it also keeps me feeling well in my head due to the release of all those amazing hormones during exercise. Keeping fit through exercising most days is the top tool in my toolkit. I am so lucky and blessed that I get to do this as a job and I have total respect for everyone out there who fits exercise into their lives on top of a job, running a house and all the many other things that they are required to do.

One of the great things that I have seen come out of lockdown is the number of people who have taken up some form of exercise. Whether it's a daily walk or run, a home exercise class or an online PT session, lots of people are finding a love for fitness that they just did not have before.

Within twenty-four hours of going back to my daily routines and practices, I felt myself returning to the ME that I most like to be. I would love to say that I will never fall off the wagon again, and I will never stop these practices. I am realistic enough to recognise, however, that I am human, and to err is human and all that. It is my intention going forward, however, to forgive myself and return to the practices which I know work.

Questions for Journaling and Reflection

- What mental and physical wellbeing tools do you currently practice?

- In what way can you schedule in a daily mental and physical wellbeing practice?

- When was the last time you listened intuitively to what your body needed?

- What would you want your mental and physical wellbeing to look like in ten years' time?

New Belief Statements for The Tricks of The Trade

- I love me.

- I take the initiative to create my life the way I want it.

- It is ok for me to make mistakes.

- I am committed to making my life work.

- I forgive myself for all my faults and imperfections.

Lesson 15:
As the World Starts to Turn Again

....

Be still and know I am near you,
Be still, I am the Lord.

Journal Entry

Dear God,

Today it is my intention to:

- *Focus on me, be present, live in alignment with my purpose, trust in the process and surrender.*

- *Be present with Craig and the kids. Show them the love and gratitude I feel in my heart.*

- *Wash my hair – it's been six days, and even Dusty Dog isn't coming near me – and he sniffs the bums of other dogs.*

- *Progress through my to-do list, as that will take me closer to the achievement of my goals.*

Please help me.

All my love always,
MC xxx

Mid-June 2020, 'Your Pal Boris' made a decision to relax certain lockdown measures. This was met with a lot of criticism – and I mean A LOT. Social media was rife with opinions on what a bumbling idiot he was, how he didn't have a clue, that he was unclear in his message and that it was on his head if the number of deaths rose back up again.

The good people of the UK turned on him; he was no longer the hero of the hour, the saviour. It reminded me of how the crowds turned on Jesus and asked Pontius Pilot to release the mad serial killer Barabbas and crucify Jesus instead – even though the week before they all thought that Jesus was the bees-knees.

Watching this from a distance (on account of me having stopped the excessive news watching and only tapping into the main headlines) made me sad. Despite all the time that we have had to self-reflect, to notice the things that we would like to change about ourselves. Despite the teachings that have been put on a plate for us during this time. Despite the opportunity that we have had to return to what God truly wants for us, the return to loving ourselves, loving our neighbour and loving the world, a lot of the human race has either missed the lesson, misunderstood the lesson, or understood it and chosen not to live by it.

The Scottish First Minister, Nicola Sturgeon then announced three weeks after Boris did that she is starting to relax the lockdown measures. For the past three weeks, those of us that live in Scotland have been doing things differently from England, and the relaxed measures that the UK government introduced were not introduced in Scotland on account of the Scottish government believing that we needed to keep the stringent measures in place for a little longer to contain the virus and push the R number down.

The R number details how many other people a person who is infected with the virus could spread it to if they came into contact with others. They want to keep this R number below 1, as this will then reduce the spread of the virus.

The R number confuses me a bit.

The relaxation of the measures included being able to meet people from one other family outside – at a park or in a garden, so long as social distancing measures are adhered to, and there are no more than eight people at the gathering. Other measures are that non-essential outdoor businesses can re-open and that people can meet to engage in outdoor physical activity, so long as there is no contact. She mentioned golf and outdoor swimming.

When the relaxation measures were announced, it seemed like everyone around me was rejoicing, celebrating that the world was beginning to go back to normal.

Everyone apart from me, that is.

I absolutely loved the lockdown time, being safe in my bubble, feeling protected from the big bad world. I didn't believe that I was ready to jump back on my hamster wheel and start furiously running faster and faster, aiming for a destination that I am not even sure that I want to get to. I didn't know if I was ready to put myself into situations where I felt that I have to be someone different in order to fit it, to do jobs that I felt were pointless and brought me absolutely no joy whatsoever.

I did not want to have to spend precious time away from the people who I love with all my heart and soul, and, selfishly, I didn't want them to have to be away from me. When I thought about Craig having to go back to his office – leaving at 8 am, not coming home until 6 pm, us passing like ships in the night, as I am out teaching classes until 8 pm – it filled me with dread, and I could physically feel myself pulling back from it, resisting it, willing and wishing it all to go away.

And then I remembered, I am not the same person coming out of lockdown as I was going into it. I have a new self-awareness. I have been taught many lessons, and as a result of learning these lessons, I now know that I get to create how my life shapes up to be. I get to choose what I do on a daily basis, and I get to decide whether I am going to return to my previous occupation of professional plate-spinner and hamster-wheel-turner. It is actually up to me. If I have learned any lesson at all during the period of lockdown, it is that the world will not fall out of the sky if I am not working 24/7 and that my family will not be living in a cardboard box out in the street if I am not out hustle, hustle, hustling for work and saying yes to every single job opportunity that is offered to me.

I recognised that what actually needed to be addressed was what future did I want to create? What would fill me with joy going forward, with a sense of excitement to get back out there in the world doing what I love and loving what I do?

Creating a future which fulfils all our desires begins with defining what our purpose is. Once we define this, we can then look at whether we are living in alignment with this purpose. We can assess how satisfied or dissatisfied we are with how we are showing up in the world.

We can create our future vision.

I took the time to define how I wanted my life to look post-lockdown.

I gave myself the gift of granting myself the time to decide what a fulfilled and happy life would really look like for me.

Establishing what is it that my heart truly desires.

Completing the following steps really helps gain clarity on what we want from life and what we want to create going forward.

Establish Our Purpose

By spending some time going inward, listening to my inner God-voice, and really exploring what I was put on this planet for was the first step in gaining clarity over what I wanted my life to look like, as opposed to allowing it up to the winds of chance. I really explored what I feel and believe in my heart I was destined to be, do and have.

Was it to be an incredible parent? A brilliant cook? The person who made everyone pee their pants laughing? The individual who helped to reduce world poverty?

It could have been a combination of these things; it could have been something completely different.

I trusted whatever came up for me, and I wrote it down. Knowing that this is the thing that everything should lead back to. This is what keeps us on track when life starts to get in the way again.

I believe my purpose is to live fully as a child of God, loving myself, my neighbour, and the world, inspiring others to look after themselves mentally and physically.

Create an Inventory

Now that my purpose was clear, it was time to look at where I was currently, looking at what makes up my world and assessing how satisfied I am with the various different elements.

Until we really explore how much we are giving to various aspects of our life and establishing how much joy we are receiving in return for the input of energy, we might not realise that we could be putting a whole lot of attention into things that do not serve us well. Things that are not in alignment with our purpose.

I used the following exercise to help me with my inventory.

Exercise

1 - Create a list of everything that makes up your world. Some areas which could be listed are Family, Finances, Work, Health, Spirituality, Self-Care and Hobbies.

2 - Add things which are important to you that aren't currently on this list but should be. For instance, do you crave more 'me time', or would you like to learn a new skill? Whatever you feel is missing, jot it down.

3 - Now rate each area in terms of how satisfied you are from 1-10, 1 being completely dissatisfied to 10 being completely and utterly satisfied. Trust your gut, your inner wisdom, and your intuition with this and try not to overthink it.

4 - The next step is to go deeper, to really explore the reasons behind the satisfaction rating you gave to each of the areas, being mindful of taking personal responsibility for the ratings. Journaling on each area is really useful and really allows you to tap into the heart of the matter.

5 - From here, you will have a clearer picture of what areas truly matter to you and what areas don't matter quite so much. This exercise creates a platform, a starting point for change where you can increase your satisfaction level with the areas which are most important to you.

Essential or Non-Essential

During the months of lockdown, the words 'essential' or 'non-essential' were used for everything. Whether it be shopping, travel, work or going outside, everything was classified as essential (yes, we can do it) or non-essential (no, we should not).

We stopped seeing our family and friends because it was classed as non-essential contact. The majority of people worked from home on account of the work they did was not determined to be essential, and travelling further than a few miles from our home was a no-no. I found it to have been a relatively easy transition, with most of us adapting to it.

We became skilled at separating the essential from the non-essential.

With this newly acquired skill, I made an intention to continue to use it going forward in my life. I am now able to boldly move forward, creating a life which will move me to a place of true happiness and inner peace.

The easiest way for me to do this is to focus my energy and attention on the essentials, and minimise doing anything which I class as non-essential. Looking at the list of areas which I determined in the previous exercise, I can ask myself whether I class the investment of my time and energy into that particular area is an essential investment. Is it in alignment with my purpose?

If it is not, then I can decide to minimise my investment of time and energy and redistribute this into activities which are in alignment with my purpose.

This period of time has been an opportunity for me to reflect and to explore what I truly want to create. No longer will I settle for doing things which are not in alignment with what I want from life.

From Purpose Comes Vision

Once I established what my purpose was and what was essential/non-essential for me to live in alignment with my purpose, I could then create a vision for the future.

A great way to do this is to create a vision board. Creating a vision board allows us to detail 'the big stuff'. How amazing would a life lived in alignment with our true purpose look?

A vision board can be in the format of one picture which captures everything you wish to create in your life, or it could be a series of visions for each separate area. The number one rule is that it must be in alignment with your purpose. It can be hand-drawn or created with pictures from magazines, etc. – whatever works best for you.

Over the years, I have created many vision boards, which detail in pictorial form what I want from life as well as what I want to contribute back to the world, with mind-blowing success.

On my vision board, the key themes are around family and friends, my connection to God and myself, my contribution to the world, and my desire to travel and have fun. All of these areas align with my true purpose.

I found it vitally important when creating my board to really feel into the vision with belief and excitement – as if it has already happened.

I then create my vision statements, which I write in the present tense – as if they have already happened or are happening just now.

Writing our vision statements in the present tense encourages the subconscious mind to see them as real, as something that we are bringing into reality. Once the vision statements are installed into the subconscious, they will work away in the background to bring them into our current reality, creating opportunities (or God-incidences, which is my favourite way to describe it) which will allow us all to have the life of our dreams.

Once the vision board and vision statements are created, it is important to look at them daily, reaffirming to the subconscious mind that this is what we truly want from life. A good way to do this is to sit in quiet meditation, focusing on the vision board. This, along with writing down my vision statements every day, really helps me to feel into my vision with excitement and belief.

SMART Goals

The next step is to break the vision into SMART goals.

I try to make my goals SMART – a time old method which has been used in business and life for as long as I can remember – with a few twists. As opposed to standing for Specific, Measurable, Achievable, Realistic, and Time-bound, I like to make my goals Spiritually-driven, Mind-blowing, Attainable, Risky, and True to You.

Spiritually Driven

The Big Guy looks favourably on goals that are for the greater good of the world. A goal which will have a positive impact on your life, the life of others' close to you and the world as a whole is always a good goal to set.

Mind-blowing

The achievement of a goal should be so exciting that it slightly blows your mind. It should also be a life-changing experience in that when the goal is achieved, life will never be the same again – for the better.

Attainable

The subconscious mind likes to work on bringing things to fruition which it truly believes that, with a bit of effort, can actually be done. When creating goals, it is important to have some form of belief that the goal can actually happen – even just the tiniest belief will be enough.

Risky

With all that said about being attainable – there has to be a feeling that you would have to stretch yourself out of your comfort zone to achieve it. You should feel excited and slightly nervous when thinking about it.

True to you

There is absolutely no point whatsoever setting a goal which is not in true alignment with who you are at your core and what your purpose is. Again, the Big Guy will see through this BS, and the chances are it just will not happen.

Release with Trust and Belief

Here is the part that confused me for a long time, and I truly believe that I have only really GOT it during the period of lockdown where I had the chance to get really clear on my purpose, vision, and goals.

Once I put in all that effort defining my purpose, then breaking it down into a big picture vision, followed by spending the time taking the vision onto the next stage through the creation of SMART goals – it was then a key requirement to detach myself from the outcome and sit in gratitude with what I currently have in my life.

Confused? Yes, so was I! For a long time, my belief was that I needed to think about my goals all the time, fixate on them and focus on them happening. This then led to frustration, dissatisfaction and worry that my goals would never be realised. And, as the age-old saying, 'You bring about what you think about,' goes, guess what I brought into my reality? You guessed it – frustration, dissatisfaction and worry.

The reason this was happening was that I was trying to achieve my goals consciously – I was trying to control, force and manage the whole process. What I have learned through studying the power of the subconscious mind during lockdown is that amazing things are created when we hand the steering wheel over to a force higher than ourselves – the force of God.

Incredible things are given to us when our hearts are filled with love and gratitude for what we currently have in our lives.

When you think about it, it takes a whole lot of the pressure off of us in terms of consciously trying to achieve our goals. The process of creating a life we truly deserve involves us determining our purpose, creating a vision and breaking the vision down into small manageable chunks.

The next part is releasing with trust and belief that our goals will be brought into reality (or something better is coming along), taking action and opportunities when they are presented to us, and living the life we currently have with gratitude and love.

Pop on Our Big Girl Pants

All of the above sounds like a breeze, doesn't it? Well, to put it bluntly, it's not! It is simple, but it is not easy. In order to create the life that we truly deserve and want, we often have to let go of things that, whilst they might give us a sense of safety and comfort, are holding us back. These things could be a relationship, a job, a habit or a belief.

We have to spring clean our lives, saying goodbye to the old to make space for the new.

When I trained as a coach, one of the key teachings which really resonated with me was, 'To let go, to let come,' which says it all, really. Until we create space in our lives to let new, exciting opportunities in, then the new, exciting opportunities simply won't come along.

I made an intention post-lockdown to be brave, to live in alignment with my purpose and vision, and to let go of all things which do not serve me or the world.

I popped on my Big Girls Pants.

Questions for Journaling and Reflection

- What is your life purpose, your reason for being put here?

- What non-essential activities are you currently spending energy on?

- What is your big picture, five-year vision?

- Create three to five SMART goals from this vision.

New Belief Statements for As the World Starts to Turn

- I take the initiative to create my life the way that I want it.

- I am true to my personal vision.

- I am a powerful, valuable person.

- I give myself permission to do what I love.

- I am willing to take the risks needed to live an incredible life.

Lesson 16:
Live in the Now

....

'Live the moment as if today is all
we truly have and believe in your heart
that something wonderful is about to happen.'

Journal Entry

Dear God,

I am so grateful for the night-time prayer habit that Charlotte and I started since I returned from Rome. It is truly special, and I love how her quirkiness shines through when she says, 'Please help me to sleep safe, comfortable, cold, protected in your love and please help all the other children in the world. Help them to sleep safe, comfortable, whatever temperature they want, protected in your love. All my love always, Charlotte.'

I am so bloody lucky to have been blessed with the life I have. Thank you thank you thank you.

All my love always – and if I could also be cold (damn hot flushes), that would be awesome.

MC xxx

Gerry Cinnamon, in my opinion, is a modern-day prophet. The Rumi of the music world. Wise beyond his years, deep as the ocean and inspirational beyond measure. His lyrics are filled with so many golden nuggets that have lifted and guided me along the path of enlightenment on many an occasion.

It was announced about a month into lockdown that Gerry Cinnamon was rescheduling his July gig at Hampden Stadium. I was devastated about it, and it was a tough blow on my global pandemic emotional rollercoaster. Now, I know that a cancelled gig is not that important in the big scale of things – hundreds of thousands of people were losing their lives, often alone and without the proper send-off that they deserve. Please hear me out, however.

The Gerry gig gave me HOPE. A hope, belief, trust and a knowing that this craziness was all eventually going to go away in a relatively short space of time. I got that we have been made to stop, get off our respective hamster wheels, reflect, learn our lessons and afterwards the world would start turning again. We would merrily get on with our lives after a couple of months of lockdown.

This does not look at all like it will be the case, judging by the number of things that are being cancelled for many months to come.

This is how the Gerry gig played out in my mind.

It is Saturday the 18th of July 2020, and I have woken up naturally after a beautiful, restful nights' sleep with a huge smile on my face and an inner knowing that it was a gorgeously sunny day outside. I would turn to see if Craig was awake, and he would turn to me with the same happy, excited smile. We would, ahem, 'cuddle', and set ourselves up for a good day.

Craig would get up and bring me a coffee in bed before taking Dusty Dog for a walk, and I would lie in bed doing a bit of meditation and journaling before heading downstairs to make eggs and toast for everyone's breakfast.

The kids would come down, every single one of them in a brilliant mood, and we would sit at the breakfast bar, with Gerry songs playing on Alexa, enjoying each other's company. The kids would be excited as they were going to the caravan with my mum and dad and their three cousins (two human and one of the furry variety). The chat would be about swimming in the sea and who was having which bodyboard.

After breakfast, the kids would get ready, and Craig would take them and Dusty Dog to my mum's. I would head to the shower and then the hairdressers, where I would get a funky festival style done in my hair. My hair would have been recently coloured following lockdown, and I would have my bright blond and vibrant purple peek-a-boo underlayer going on. The chat in the salon would be flowing, with a lot of customers also heading into Glasgow for the concert. As we sit getting our hair styled, we would discuss how we were getting through, where we were going beforehand, whether we were sitting or standing, who was supporting him and how excited we were for this first outdoor gig after lockdown.

We would say how it was going to be a BELTER (the name of the song which launched his commercial career, for all the non-fans). The bubble of happiness, connection and excitement in my stomach would be growing and growing, and I would be feeling this palpable buzzing force of positive energy coursing through and out of me. It would feel amazing.

Back home, I would do my make-up and get dressed in a cracking new outfit, bought especially for the gig. Bought from an actual real live shop, which I was able to go into without fear of touching anything or being terrified of getting close to another human being who was not in my family. No longer under the watchful eye of a poor shop assistant who had the remit added to their job description of only allowing a certain amount of people into the shop and giving anyone who does not follow the flow arrows or tries to buy more than three items of anything a warning.

Craig and I would compliment each other on how great we were looking – both feeling amazing. The excitement and happiness would go up another notch. As we leave the house, we would lock up saying our usual, 'You got the key?' to which one of us would sing, 'I got the key, I got the secret!' Cheesy, I know, but it keeps us amused.

We would head to our local town where we would meet our 'Festival Buddies' – our besties who we go to most gigs and festivals with. There would be cuddles, kisses, the chat would be flowing, more cuddles, kisses and general sending of the menfolk to the bar for drinks. We would be loving life, loving each other's company – in our own wee festival buddies bubble. The excite-o-meter would go up another level. Woooooo hoooooooo.!

On the train heading through to Glasgow, we would have, as us Scottish folk call it, 'a carry oot' – which is basically alcohol which you drink outside or take to a house party. There would be snacks (of the healthy and non-healthy variety), and someone would start a sing-song. Obviously, singing Gerry songs. I would look out the window mindfully, taking all this in – experiencing feelings of deep connection and gratitude for my life, for my family and friends and for the shining of the sun. It would be magical.

On our arrival in Glasgow, we would head to the stadium, taking in a few pubs along the way. Meeting old friends and making new – everyone in a BELTER of a mood, and everyone out to achieve the same thing – to have an amazing time and make fantastic memories.

Up ahead, Hampden would come into view. A glorious vision against the backdrop of the sun starting to lower in the sky. The excitement and expectation would be building and building in all of us – everyone would feel it, and everyone would be ready for the gig of their lives!

We would all enter as a collective, grab a couple of beers each and walk down the stairs onto the pitch. We would find an amazing spot with a cracker of a view of the stage, within an easy distance of toilet and bar facilities (this is vitally important, as anyone who has ever been to a gig with me will already know).

The sun would be going down, dusk would settle, the support act would finish, the air would be filled with green, blue, pink and red smoke from smuggled-in flares and then it would start…………

Dum de dum dum de dum de dum.

The opening chords of Sweet Caroline. The song that is ALWAYS played before Gerry comes on. The excite-o-meter would be off the scale, everyone would be taking deep breaths, trying to keep a lid on the euphoric experience they would be having. No-one would need to say a word – we would all know what's coming and we would be ready for it. There would be knowing smiles and meaningful looks all around and as we all finish singing 'Sweet Caroline', the man himself would walk onto the stage………………..and start…………

Except all of that isn't going to happen.

To say I was gutted when it was announced is an understatement. The Gerry gig had been my Mecca, my light at the end of the tunnel. It was the one thing that I held onto during the lockdown period.

And it was cancelled.

I gave myself the full day following the announcement to be grumpy, withdrawn and sad – leaning into the feeling that all hope was gone, as opposed to denying, deferring or suppressing, which were my previous, go-to, default choice of actions when I felt low.

I went to my bed in a huff. In bed, I did what I always do during my dark days. I asked God for help and assistance in learning whatever lesson I am being asked to learn.

At this point, the girls came up and climbed into bed with me, very bravely, given my mood, to cuddle into me, making a 'Mummy Sandwich', with me in the middle.

At the side of my bed, I saw the photo of me as a small girl, about four or five years old. I saw I was in a playpark, on a climbing frame. I had a beautiful blue dress on, and the biggest smile on my face. Charlotte reached over, picked this up and handed it to me, asking me lots of questions about it, in the way that only Charlotte can. When was it taken? Who took the photo? Why was I wearing such an awful dress? And for what reason was I wearing socks with open-toed sandals?

After answering all her questions, I looked deep into little-girl-me's eyes and saw, maybe for the first time, complete and utter HOPE shining out of them. Hope for an amazing future, filled with endless possibilities and excitement.

It hit me then that I couldn't possibly have lost this hope that I was born with because I wasn't going to get to a live concert for a while. I mean, I still kept a hold of HOPE and belief, despite all the many major challenges and knockdowns that I have faced and overcome over the years.

I was born with hope and a belief that everything will work out well in the end, and I realised when looking at the picture of little me that, whilst it is lovely to look forward to things in the future, you cannot and should not attach everything to it. You should not put all your eggs in one basket, as they say.

And just like little me had hope and a belief that the future would be filled with endless possibilities and excitement, I realised then that forty-five-year-old me does too. What is different is that little me was completely and utterly happy having a blast in the present moment – having fun in a playpark, whereas forty-five-year-old me was making it about the future, which is never guaranteed to be exactly as we plan it to be.

And then it hit me – I had moved my attention from appreciating, accepting and being grateful for the here and now, and was looking too far into the future – a future that, despite the best-laid plans, is never guaranteed.

With that realisation, in that very moment, my focus shifted, and I looked at what was happening in the here and now. I was in the middle of a gorgeously tasty mummy sandwich with the most incredible daughters that anyone could ever ask for. I was surrounded by love, I was connected (albeit virtually) most days to my festival buddies, and I had hope and belief that Hampden in the sun with Gerry headlining would happen – exactly when it is meant to.

Questions for Journaling and Reflection

- What am I truly grateful for in this moment?

- What can I think about right now that will lift my vibration?

- What did I learn about myself today?

- What is beautiful about today?

New Belief Statements for Living in the Now

- I see beauty in all aspects of my life.

- I am present.

- I experience harmony in mind, body and spirit.

- I am exactly where I am meant to be.

- I am learning my lessons with love.

Lesson 17:
The Healing Energy of the
Summer Solstice

....

May the long-time Sun
Shine upon you,
All love surround you,
And the pure light within you
Guide your way on.

Journal Entry

Dear God,

Please please please please make Ciaran be ok.

All my love always,
MC xxx

On Saturday the 21st of June 2020, the longest day of the year, I ended up in St John's Hospital, whilst Ciaran, my man-child, had just been returned from the operating theatre. It was the last place in the world at this current period of time that we wanted to be; however, it is what it is.

It all started after dinner the previous evening when Ciaran was doing his chores. It is his responsibility to tidy up the kitchen, empty and fill the dishwasher, and take the bins out. Doing chores is not Ciaran's preferred thing to do – he would much rather be upstairs, plugged into his PlayStation, yelling at his pals, who have allegedly done something incredibly stupid, which has resulted in him being killed on Fortnite.

Ciaran likes to rush through what he has to do in as little time as possible and often tries to get his sisters to help, much to their annoyance. Dinnertime can be such a joyful time in our household – not!

The night started off no different to any other night: we all had dinner. Craig and I had chilli chicken, and the kids had fish, chip, peas and cucumber (I am completely OCD about them having at least two veg with every meal, regardless of whether said vegetables complement each other or not).

Craig and I had planned a quiet, digital-detox evening – no work, no phones, a tub of salted caramel ice cream and an intention to watch a movie. It had been a pretty full-on week with work, home-schooling, studying and general lockdown, and I had recognised the early signs of mental and physical burnout in myself.

I have felt the burn of burnout more times than I care to remember over the last few years, and I did not want to fall headfirst into being an emotional, grouchy and exhausted individual.

We were congratulating ourselves on being able to retire to the couch by 6.45 pm – something that is unheard of generally in the Donnelly household. Common expressions that are bandied about our house and can be heard at least five times per week are, 'I can't believe that's 9 pm and that's us just sitting down,' and 'One episode of (insert boxset of the moment) and then let's get to bed.' It's a rock n roll lifestyle, let me tell you.

As I was snuggling my phone up to bed for the evening and wondering how long I should leave the ice cream before it was that perfect consistency – not too runny and not too much of an effort on the spoon – I heard one word from Ciaran. The word 'Mum'. Just 'Mum', and on hearing that one word in the tone that it was said, everything went into slow-motion and became really quiet, exactly like it did during Benji-gate.

In this slow space, my mother's intuition kicked in, and I just knew deep inside me that something wasn't right, that something not good had happened. I turned to look at my boy, and there he was, blood dripping from his hand. He had turned a funny colour and had walked over to the sink, turned on the tap, and was attempting to clean the blood away – his own intuition guiding him subconsciously towards the right thing for him to do.

Everything then became really fast and blurry and looking back on it now, I can't actually recall exactly what fully happened and in what sequence. It was a combination of Craig taking control of calming Ciaran down, the girls giggling nervously trying to make light of it (as only little sisters can), and me googling everything from 'Can you present to A&E without an appointment during coronavirus' to 'How to treat a deep cut on the hand', whilst calling NHS24, my mum, and my sister – trying to work out the best solution for the situation.

We established the cause of blood when clearing the kitchen after dinner. Ciaran had been pressing rubbish into an already full bin (on account of trying to make a speedy return to the Fortnite competition he was in the middle of prior to dinner). Queue rolly-eyed Mother.

The extra thirty seconds it would have required to take the bin out to the main bin outside was just not worth it.

When pressing the rubbish down into the full bin, Ciaran's hand made an unfortunate connection with an empty tin of tomatoes or kidney beans from the chilli chicken, which resulted in slicing his left hand open at the bottom of his little finger. The cut was so deep, and when I eventually plucked up the courage to look at it, I immediately feared that he was going to lose his finger.

One of our neighbours who is a nurse kindly came over to look at it and confirmed that it would need treatment as it was so deep, and given that Ciaran had no feeling in it, the nerve might have been damaged.

Off to Accident and Emergency we nervously popped.

On entering the hospital, I encouraged Ciaran to draw down his bell jar whilst I pulled mine over us to protect us from any invisible nasties that might be lurking around in the hospital. A few of my friends work in the hospital, and they had advised me that if a visit to the hospital could be avoided, then it should be and that the media is only telling the public half the story. The illness, pain and death that they are seeing on a daily basis has taken its toll on their mental and physical wellbeing.

You can imagine my apprehension having to take my boy there.

Thankfully, the Accident & Emergency department was very quiet, and I can only commend the staff there for their professionalism and speed in dealing with Ciaran. Unfortunately, however, given the severity of the cut, we were advised that we would need to return the following morning for him to be seen by a specialist in plastic surgery, as it looked like the nerve was indeed damaged and he would need an operation.

We returned home, nervous again about having to return the next day.

On returning to the hospital the next morning, I again initiated our bell jars, and I asked for God's protection and for the best possible outcome for Ciaran. We were asked to make a base in the children's ward, after some double-checking of his date of birth, and exclamations of, 'Oh my, fifteen? I would serve you a drink in a pub!' Ciaran looks a lot older than his years.

The surgeon came, examined him, and again confirmed that there was nerve damage and that he would need an operation to repair the nerve and stitch up the wound. His recommendation was that it would be better if this procedure was done under general anaesthetic.

Shortly after this, he was gowned and prepped for theatre.

I was nervous, and my mother's intuition was strongly guiding me that this was not the best possible outcome for my boy. I leaned in, trusted in God and the process, and accepted that it would all be ok and that we would be looked after. All over social media, I was being reminded that it was the longest day of the year – the summer solstice – and that we were being surrounded by an incredible healing energy. A great time for release, acceptance and manifesting miracles.

A healing miracle, in my opinion, was exactly what occurred.

My friend Alison sent me a message to send her love and to tell me that she was sending theta healing Ciaran's way. As soon as I had read her message, the surgeon re-entered the room to say that on account of the anaesthetists being extremely busy in theatre, would Ciaran be ok with having the procedure done under local anaesthetic?

My heart breathed a sigh of relief. My intuition said, 'Yes, this is for Ciaran's highest good.' I quickly texted Alison back, telling her that it was working, that Ciaran was no longer getting a general anaesthetic, asking her to keep sending the healing energy.

Very quickly afterwards, Ciaran was taken to theatre to have the procedure. I walked him down, gave him all my love and returned to base camp to pray for the best possible outcome.

Within what felt like minutes, he was returned to me, and I was told that he was ok. The surgeon was delighted to report that there was no nerve damage, and the tendon was fine. He had stitched up the wound, and the feeling would return to Ciaran's finger after a couple of days.

Alleluia, Alleluia – the best possible outcome did occur. The power of prayer, theta healing, a summer solstice and a bloody good national health service worked a miracle. Within one hour, we were out of the hospital, having been through the golden arches, and Ciaran was happily munching on a burger, eagerly anticipating a chore-free afternoon spent shouting at his friends about Fortnite.

The lesson I learned that day was to never underestimate mother's intuition, the power of prayer, and the universal healing energy which is available to us always.

Questions for Journaling and Self-Reflection

- In what ways can you tap into the healing energy which is available to us all?

- What does complete mental and physical health look like for you?

- Who needs you to send healing energy their way?

- In what ways can you become a healer?

New Belief Statements for Healing

- My body heals itself naturally and quickly.

- I nurture myself in healthy and loving ways.

- I trust in the universal healing energy which is available to me.

- I trust that I am being looked after.

- I am safe and trusting during the healing process.

Lesson 18:
This is the Beginning of the
Rest of Your Life

....

Give me love in my heart, keep me serving
Give me love in my heart, I pray
Give me love in my heart, keep me serving
Keep me serving till the break of day

Journal Entry

Dear God,

Thank you so much for the healing, acceptance, forgiveness and release that took place during my QEC session tonight. A miracle has occurred, for which I am so grateful. I feel lighter, unburdened, forgiven and untethered to the situation which has held me back for so long. I see things differently now. I see myself differently now. I am love, I am light, I have learned my lessons.

Thank you,

All my love always,
MC xxx

Towards the end of June 2020, I sat in silence looking out the window of my Ploffice (a Donnelly term for a combined playroom and office – previously known as the garage) at the driving wind and rain. I remember thinking that I could not believe how hot, sunny and lovely the Scottish weather was the previous week. The temperature had reached the mid-20's and the whole nation was in 'taps-aff' mode, loving life and BBQ-ing everything that could be justifiably BBQ'd.

Scottish people are a strange breed. On the one hand, we crave nice weather and moan constantly about the rain that we get 350 days of the year, yet when we do get some warm weather, we moan about how it is roasting and that we cannot get a breath. And please don't get us started on how we couldn't get a decent night's sleep on account of it being so hot (and not of the wink-wink hot variety).

Or maybe that is just me, on account of my 'ginger skin', as Craig has always referred to it. Many years ago, early on in our relationship, he went into a shop to buy me skincare. When the shop assistant asked him what my skin type was, he told her it was 'ginger'. The cuteness of this still makes me laugh now.

It's now mid-November 2020, and I sit in the same seat in my Ploffice, looking out again at the driving rain and wind. No-one has had their 'taps aff' for weeks now, and we are all moaning about how cold it is and how dark it is at 4 pm. Scottish people talk about the weather, A LOT!!

The news this week suggests that certain parts of Scotland will be entering into Level 4 – the new name for lockdown (don't get me started). I thought it would be all over by now, that we would all be going about our daily lives, pretty much having returned to how we were at the start of the year. It looked as if it was going to be all over. The numbers were going down to an acceptably low level, the hospitality and beauty industry opened back up, and Joanna and I got to gleefully reopen our gym, welcoming all our amazing clients back with open arms (being mindful not to hug them, on account of the social distancing measures which were still in place).

People were allowed to travel outside of their region, and Craig and I enjoyed a wonderful weekend in London – just the two of us, enjoying each other's company and the fact the it was cocktail week in London– hellooooo, Aperol Spritz.

Six weeks later – our gym had to close again, as did the pubs and restaurants. The virus is still here, stronger than ever. Numbers are rising daily, and people are losing the fight against it and being taken from this world. Hospitals are at capacity, and people are fearful that this will never end. There is so much that is out of our control, and I am being reminded of the lesson to focus on what I can control – my mind, my body and what I place my attention on. My mantra of 'Right now, I am ok' is back on its repeat loop to remind me that right now, I am ok.

I am choosing to see this as a further opportunity to continue to learn and grow – as being granted the time to face my shadow self and have the space to release and heal the next layer.

During lockdown this year, I was able to train to become a fully qualified Quantum Energy Coach. I have learned and been reminded of so much during this training, and I have been inspired by the teachings of Dr Bruce Lipton, Dr Joe Dispenza, Brene Brown and Gabor Mate, to name just a few.

For me, Quantum Energy Coaching has felt like the missing piece of the puzzle. The Holy Grail for creating the life that I truly desire and deserve. The modality which enables us to let go of all our past conditioning, stories and beliefs which are not serving us and allows us to open up to the possibility of creating and manifesting an incredible future.

A future where we love ourselves, love our neighbour and love our world. Just as God intended for us.

The final teachings on the course were around manifestation and how it was possible to bring into your reality whatever your heart truly desired – with the provision that it was for the greater good of the world. We were taught that in order to create our dream life, we first have to remove the blocks which are holding us back. Once these blocks are removed and the slate is wiped clean, we can remember that this day is indeed the beginning of the rest of our lives. We can be, do and have whatever our heart desires – living in alignment with what we are truly here for. What God intended for us. We can live from a place of purpose and excitement.

Stepping into this bright, shiny new future can be metaphorically likened to threading a needle – with us assuming the role of the piece of thread.

A thread cannot be passed through the eye of a needle if it is knotted and tangled – it would get stuck. When all the knots are removed, the thread can easily slip through the eye and come out the other side freely. And just like the thread, we cannot live an incredible life filled with love, joy, peace and happiness if we still have knots which need to be removed.

Over the weeks of lockdown, I was granted the opportunity to identify so many knots in my thread. I have been blessed with the chance to untangle them by doing the necessary inner work required. I have done this by identifying many limiting beliefs, based on past conditioning which I have attributed meaning to and stories which I have created in my mind.

I am so grateful to have had this time to do the inner work, the unknotting of the thread. With the completion of my shadow work, I will feel ready to pass easily and freely through the eye of the needle to the other side. The side where life is easy, abundant in all I need and want, following my bliss each and every day. I am feeling it happening already. It feels incredible.

We need to do the inner work; we need to unknot the thread. It is one of the crucial elements in creating an incredible future. God intended for us all to live an easy, free and connected life, doing the things that we love. Why on earth would He intend anything else for us?

What sort of God would He be if He gifted us with life and then expected us to strive and struggle from the day we were born, having to put in so much effort into getting what our hearts desired?

To live our dream life, we must unknot the thread. The thread which we allowed, through no fault of our own or blame of others, to become knotted. It is so important to show up consistently, putting in the work and effort required, to free us up to pass easily into the blissful flow of life where we are vibrating at such a high frequency. The frequency of gratitude, love and connection.

The knots which I have worked really hard to undo during this lockdown period include the knot of not feeling good enough, as well as the knot of feeling that I had to hide certain sides of myself. I have also untangled the knots of not loving myself completely, being fearful of judgement (which included an extra knot of people-pleasing), and being afraid to fail.

I am so thankful to God for granting me this space to unknot my thread, and I am grateful to myself for loving myself enough to do it. I have done the inner work required consistently during this period of time; I have really dug deep, explored, accepted, and came out the other side loving all of me a whole lot more.

I have learnt so many lessons, and I make it my intention to remember them, moving forward towards my dreams, towards living a life which I truly believe that we all deserve. A life filled with everything our hearts desire. Love, connection, inner peace, growth, and so much fun.

The life that God intended for us all.

Going forward, I will grant myself permission to live a life on my terms, free from guilt, people-pleasing, beating myself up, and feeling less-than.

I am so grateful to myself for taking this time during lockdown to call out my old beliefs and stories and working on installing new, better-serving beliefs. I feel lighter, more positive and freer than I have ever done in my life. I look forward to working with and inspiring others to do the same through sharing these lessons because every single person on this planet deserves to live an incredible life.

Finally, I am excited (and a little bit scared) to step forward into this next phase with an understanding that I still have many more lessons to learn.

Because life is like that, isn't it? The continual learning of lessons is necessary and enables us to continually grow, create and contribute on a massive scale.

It's about learning to love the journey.

Do the work, show up for yourself every day, love all of you, commit to releasing the stories and limiting beliefs, and finally, have unwavering faith in God.

I hope this has made some kind of sense.

Amen x

Questions for Journaling and Reflection

- Am I creating the life of my dreams?

- Do I show up for myself every single day?

- Are there any remaining knots which need to be released?

- What lessons have I learnt today?

New Belief Statements for This is the Beginning of The Rest of Your Life

- I am learning my lessons with love.

- I am committed to manifesting my life's purpose.

- I dare to allow my visions and dreams to come true.

- I give myself permission to do what I love.

- I am committed to making my life work.

Epilogue

....

So, there you have it, the lessons I was given by God during lockdown.

My WISH is that anyone who reads them and completes the journaling and affirmation exercises will gain so many insights, which will enable them to return to feeling happier, healthier and with more self-belief as a result.

My ultimate DREAM is that whoever reads them will feel more connected to God's love and will tap into the infinite protection and blessing that it brings.

You will remember that whilst we were in Rome prior to lockdown, my sister Gillian was none too pleased to have been divinely guided into St Peter's Cathedral for holy mass with Pope Francis – especially more so when she found out that she would be in there for over two hours and the only wine that would be available would be of the communion variety.

My sister Gillian is the funniest person I have ever met – she has me in stitches with tears running down my face all the time. She is the most beautiful soul – kind, loving, compassionate, and the best friend anyone could ever ask for.

She also lacks faith in God, something that we have had to agree to disagree about over the years.

Gillian was the first person I allowed to read this book. I trusted her to be honest with her feedback and praise – I knew that she would tell me exactly what she thought of it and make suggestions for improvements where necessary. She is an avid reader, and I was both excited and nervous about her feedback, given that the book is in essence about God and His love for us all.

One night, Gillian called with feedback, and in her usual hilarious way, she told me that she had been reading my book and had a bone to pick with me. I was instantly worried. Given that a lot of the book was written in a state of flow, I wondered whether I had written something that might have inadvertently offended her.

She proceeded to tell me that after reading the book, she was mindlessly scrolling online and read that one of her friends was in a spot of trouble. She said that when she read it, she immediately, unconsciously bowed her head, brought her hands together in prayer, and said, 'Dear God, please help…………..'

She finished by saying, 'And that has only happened because of your bloody book!'

YES – My work here is done!!

Acknowledgements

....

From the bottom of my heart, I want to thank my husband Craig for showing me nothing but love and support during the years we have been together – especially more so during the time I was writing this book. You allowed me to create space to write and encouraged me to have fun during the process. Love you always. You are my soulmate and I will always be your Jaykay Rowling.

For my kids – Ciaran, Maria, and Charlotte – who have taught me many, many lessons, not just during lockdown, but every single day, thank you! I love you with all my heart and soul and always will. You are my reason for being, and I have the best job in the world – the job of being your mum.

A special thanks also to my Tribe – my mum and two sisters, Gillian and Joanna. I am so lucky and blessed to have a family who are also my best friends. You were there when this all began, and that made it even more special. I am so excited for all the other adventures we still have to go on.

An acknowledgement also to the legend that is my Dad – you have taught me many lessons over the years – the most important one being that hard work and effort pays off – as well as keeping it real. Thank you.

Thanks also go to Sean and the team from That Guy's House, especially Jo for you outstanding service, Jesse for editing my book and Leah for cover design. Reading your email Sean, where you told me that you would love to be my publisher, goes down as one of the happiest and proudest moments of my life. Thank you all for your advice, your authenticity, and your belief in me.

Last but by no means least, thank you, God, for blessing me with this incredible life and for giving me the job of writing this book. It is an honour to be able to deliver your message to those who are in need of it.

About the Author

....

Marie-Claire is an accredited Life and Quantum Energy Coach, the proud co-owner of Dream Fitness, and has created her own range of Dream Magic Superfood Powder blends which she sells and ships all over the world. She also has a passion and love for writing.

She is from West Lothian, Scotland and is married to her Craigy-Boy. Together they have three amazing cherubs and a Dusty Dog!

As you can probably guess, Marie-Claire is super passionate about all things related to health and happiness improvement. She makes a daily intention to feel buzzing with energy and vitality, and her mission in life is to enable people to be their best and feel their best – EVERY SINGLE DAY!

Marie-Claire truly believes that when you show up for yourself and fully commit to working on yourself, then you will create the life you deserve. A life filled with abundance, fulfilment, connection, and love.

Connect with Marie-Claire and learn more:
lifecoach-directory.org.uk/lifecoaches/marie-claire-donnelly

facebook.com/DreamFitnessWL
facebook.com/dreammagic07

instagram.com/dreammagicblends/
instagram.com/coachingbymc/

Lightning Source UK Ltd.
Milton Keynes UK
UKHW020119270221
379458UK00008B/245